I0453325

WHAT'S IN A LIFE

An intimate and engaging historical World War II
documented biography by an American in Nazi
and Fascist occupied Greece. Included
is the Civil War that followed.

By

Mark Athanasios C. Karras

*Greece, the first Nation to block the onslaught of the Nazi war
machine and to cause its ultimate defeat at the Russian front.*

What's in a Life
Copyright © 2017 by Athanasios C. Karras

Memoir

p. 124 (paperback)

NEW BYZANTIUM
Camarillo, CA 93010-1771

ISBN   979-8-89216-004-9 (Paperback)
           979-8-89216-005-6 (Ebook)
Library of Congress Control No. 2008923386

ALL RIGHTS RESERVED. All the material herein is protected
under the Copyright Laws of the United States. Copying of this or
any part of this material, excluding the appended WWII Defining
Quotes, without the express written authorization of its owner is
prohibited by law. 2017.

TABLE OF CONTENTS

ACKNOWLEDGEMENTS

My HEARTFELT GRATITUDE is extended to all who live and who have perished: who in World War II salvaged and preserved for humankind the preferred way of life. Such is my sentiment—my own trial during those times notwithstanding. And likewise, I give my deep love, gratitude, and honor to my parents in memory of their sacrifices, devotion, and courage in sustaining the integrity and welfare of our family throughout that dreadful period.

Special mention with my sincere gratitude goes to my friend and fine businessman Jerry Baldonado for his most valuable help in formatting and applying my manuscript to print.

PROLOGUE

CAUSE IS BEHIND EVERY symptom.

Idle and you will fail; rush and you will stumble; study and you will learn; try and you will gain; lie and you will rue; respect and you will be respected; judge and you will be judged; hate and you will be hated, love and you will be loved; and so forth. Yet with it all, in good and in bad there is time involved. And, when time is used with wisdom the outcome is more often good.

Although such are words of common sense, they are not simple in their message. They are words that spring from the heart and from wisdom that only life provides. So, let's probe ahead and visit events, which in turn caused other events that over time combined and formed part of one person's life. That person is I.

GETTING ACQUAINTED

THE FIRST EVENT TO affect me was that I was born. It was beyond doubt, and I believe everyone will agree, the most significant event ever to impact my life. Yet, in spiritual terms, I hold a serious reservation about the preeminence of that event, since my birth may only be the symptom of an earlier choice in a higher state of existence. Nevertheless, and be that as it may, I was born in 1927 in Miami, Florida. And it was once or twice with much affection that my mother had told me about her discomfort during her pregnancy with me, caused by my restlessness and recurrent kicking. I took her words to be very true, given my proclivity for action and my desire to move forward—sort of like a cork that always pops up, regardless of any restraint.

So, there I was in 1931, just four years old, when my first travel experience took place. And this is how it all happened: Both my parents were US immigrants from Greece. My father was first to arrive at Ellis Island with his older brother. Their admission into the US, as it happened, was on a second attempt; because they had both tried once before. A discrepancy in their paperwork caused them to be denied and to be returned to Greece. One must consider the emotional impact on the two youths when this occurred—my father was around eleven years old and his brother about three or four years his senior. Yet, they persisted and returned to achieve their goal. Then again, those were times when immigration laws were respected and obeyed and not ignored in the contemptuous manner witnessed today. It is strange to accept the notion that the safety of one's home should not be protected against the entry of unfamiliar strangers. Yet, it is with reckless abandon that our whole Nation is left to suffer that very danger.

Were there regrets ever expressed by my father for what he had endured? To my knowledge: None; nor were such ever alleged by anyone in the family. Quite to the contrary, my father was a proud naturalized American who felt honored to have served in the US Army in World War I, and who achieved a successful business career quite early in his life. He rose to his success having settled in Milwaukee and laboring on the railroad and in the beer industry. He used his savings to start a restaurant, but soon was advised by a lady medical doctor to consider migrating to Miami, Florida where the city was in its infancy. The move at the opening of the 1900s proved very successful. Within a brief period of time with his partners they established the well-known *Presto Restaurant* in the business center of Miami.

The Presto Restaurant on First Avenue, NE in Miami.

The place was very popular and was also patronized by prominent business and political figures. And whether this enhanced or diminished its reputation, even Al Capone ate there when he visited downtown from his plush residence on one of the islands alongside the McArthur Causeway. The fact that my father had to submit to the rigor of immigration laws, only increased his sense of respect, duty, and discipline early in his life. This did not just affect his sense of responsibility in his new country, but also pressed upon his awareness about his five unmarried sisters back home. Good judgment, conscientiousness, and effort soon won the day. Moreover, his education level in a rural setting had only reached the fourth grade. Yet, in a constant pursuit to improve his learning, he had made a self-taught effort to translate Edgar Allan Poe in Greek. He also pursued the learning of French. The trip to America was the pure symptom of family economic necessity. It was thrust upon him. His preference was to remain home and continue his education. To the dramatic surprise of his family after his departure, hidden in a niche behind the stone-built fireplace, the little boy had carved out the following painful message: "An uneducated person is an un-hewn log."

No doubt there are many around the world, young and old, who are talented and able and who wish to come to this land, and whom we wish to welcome with open arms. There must be system and order in the way this is done. The proper and productive way to do it is by the establishment, application, and conformity to rules and laws without exceptions.

Both my parents were children whose fathers were priests. By the way, it is often known that Orthodox Christianity does not demand celibacy for clergy lower than the office of bishop. The families were natives of two neighboring villages in central Greece in the Province of Phocis—the mountainous area of Delphi, Mt. Parnassus, and the coastal space of the Gulf of Corinth where the port town of Galaxidion is located. Phocians were those who guarded the secret pass in higher ground above the straight at Thermopylae. They had moved their defense position to the mountain crest. Instead, the Persians circled around the Phocians through an alternate path, having been informed by the traitor Efialtes. Historical reference has it that the settlement of Galaxidion had five sacred tombs dating back to ancient times. Many years of suffering from marauding pirates and other attacks caused some of the population to retreat to higher ground where access was much more difficult. One of those settlements was my father's village named, Pentagoi, which name can convey three different meanings: namely, Five Saints, Five Paths, or Five Sons. To date, the correct meaning has not been determined. My own opinion favors the first choice, in so far as it merits some historical connection, when thinking of the five sacred tombs. And, in my own understanding there is no particular reference that I have known of any converging five paths, or of five preeminent sons. One other thing known to me is that my paternal residence located in the center of the settlement was said to be two hundred and fifty years old in the late 1930s when our family enjoyed the summers there. The thick stone walls featured a loop-hole (narrow slit in the wall to shoot through or as an air vent) that may well have been used to defend against incursions from the Turk occupiers and others. Greece achieved its freedom in the war of 1821 to 1829, after almost four hundred years of Ottoman occupation. There is another sad contemporary sequel to all this. My father had preserved the ancient structure and had added a modern two-story stone structure with a three-level wooden porch or balcony. The third level of the porch was in effect an "eagle's nest," and all levels were accessed by a metal spiral stairway from the ground to the top. During the underground activities while the Nazis occupied Greece, a group of left-leaning guerillas bent on punishing a cousin whose property was adjacent to ours, set fire and burned everything to the ground. One of the perpetrators during the rampage, looking at our home declared, "Someone rich is here" (meaning: someone rich owns this). It seems that in his distorted sense of human equality, this was reason enough to destroy the property—sort of cutting big trees short in order that they should all look equal: a faulty symptom from a faulty cause.

(Left) My father in the US Army in 1918. (Right) My father
on the side of the stone-built extension to the ancient house
structure. All burned to the ground by partisans of the left.
Even all the collapsed stones were stolen.

My paternal grandfather served as the priest of Pentagoi to the
term of his life. His faithful dedication was countered by prolonged
economic difficulty. There is historical evidence of the community
being in arrears in meeting their church financial obligations. This,
of course, explains the demand on my father and my uncle to enter
the work force at an early age whether this was at home or abroad.
My father was the seventh child after five sisters and a brother.

My maternal grandfather served as school teacher in the
neighboring settlement, until he was ordained into the priesthood
by his acceptance and by unanimous wish of the people. He
migrated to Athens with his family and for the rest of his life
served the religious community in the vicinity where today is
located the US Embassy. The population has grown since then,
and what began with a few hundred souls, today has expanded to
hundreds of thousands with several other communities. His service
to the church included ecclesiastical judgeship at the Metropolis
of Athens of the Church of Greece. My mother was the fourth
child preceded by three brothers, one of whom perished at war,
and she was followed by three additional brothers. Their love for
their sister and in return, her love for them was profound and

well known. Furthermore, the proximity of the two settlements mentioned above and the natural interchange between the two families had as a result the union between my parents. Without doubt, my mother had been graced with the gift of physical good looks, which coupled with the presence of the young energetic and successful entrepreneur from America, formed the foundation for an excellent union. Ideals, principles, and family backgrounds were in total harmony. The promise of a good marriage was in place from the outset, and it proved to be so.

The elegant wedding ceremony that took place included many guests and the mayor of Athens as best man. No less unforgettable was the honeymoon the new couple enjoyed. It consisted first of a stay at Faliron, a coastal suburb of Athens, and continued with a colorful trip to the US in fine fashion, including hotels, class of service travel to Paris and then to the port of Cherbourg at the Anglo-American Hotel to board the luxurious *S.S. Leviathan*—at the time the biggest liner in the world—for their transatlantic crossing to New York, and then by train to Miami. The wedding took place in 1924. Business in Miami was prospering. Yet, by 1931 my mother had become quite homesick for her family in Greece. My father too had developed tender sentiments for his in-laws and for the way of life in Athens and in the countryside. His economic situation at age forty already afforded him the freedom to make the move to Greece; and he planned to travel back and forth to the US to maintain his business interests. It is without doubt that his persona throughout his stay in Greece was that of an American. Small wonder, since he had left Greece at a very young age and had grown and matured as an American. It is also important to note that in spite of my mother's brief seven-year stay in the US, her identity as well had been assimilated into the American way. She had obtained her American citizenship and had acquired aptitude in speaking, reading, and writing her new American language. Her love, admiration, and all that is American was etched deep in her heart. I witnessed this in a direct way, when once we traveled to Hawaii and during a Pearl Harbor tour of the sunken and destroyed ships (to be sure, an emotional trip for anyone); I saw her weep as a child in a heart-rending way—a sight that remains indelible in my mind. In view of all the above, in my opinion, the decision to move to Greece has but only one answer. That is, love for the family and the constant desire to be with loved ones.

MOVING ON

THE FIRST ADDITION TO our family was with the birth of my brother in 1926. Mine followed one year later; and that of the youngest, our sister, was in 1931 just prior to the family's departure for Greece. In spite of my early childhood before leaving the US, I have some very vivid memories of life in Miami. I believe that most people retain memories at a very young age, even though some may fail to bring them to the surface. This inability may occur because many folks most of their life remain in the same environment where they were born and raised. The proliferation of events within the same setting causes a memory blur by reason of repetition. In my case, the separation from my initial environment was abrupt, and so I was able to retain very vivid pictures of events that took place—that is, retaining one single snapshot at a time. Events in an unchanged environment are forever embedded in memory in one set way. Of course, the same effect would take place in very dramatic instances—the unforgettable ones, so to speak.

In any case, my experience when I returned to the US fourteen years later was astonishing. I could recall and re-capture my impressions of the surroundings as they were when I was a mere child of three or four years. To the astonishment of my godmother as well, I proceeded to describe in great detail the room arrangements of her home. The mental clutter caused by various changes over the years (and of course her indifference to remember them) had caused her to forget many details. Yet, more surprising is not the retention of the memory itself, but the age at which the human mind can gather, process, and recall information. This should encourage instilling information in very young children (but not abusing the practice), since children have the capacity to absorb and assimilate. Evidence of this capacity is present today, given the extraordinary aptitude of very young children to handle electronic devices often without instruction. Parents of young children should be aware of this, and should foster it, while at the same time making sure to encourage the wholesome social and emotional development of their children.

I cannot remember the trip from Miami to New York, but I can recall the hotel room in that city. Next, I remember the ship that ferried the family across. I can remember somehow that space was not the feature of that vessel. At least not in one instance when I was given to drink from a cup of sweetened tea with milk. I liked it so much that to this day I can still recall and enjoy its taste. And every time I drink it my mind reverts to the small room with a table and a narrow booth-like sitting arrangement. This description, of course, does not establish whether the ship was a large luxury liner or an ordinary passenger ship. The fact is that the ship was not a large one. On the other hand, it could not have been a repeat of the Leviathan, since Piraeus was not a port of call for that great ship. Second, no self-respecting patriotic Greek would want to travel to Greece other than in a Greek vessel. And third, in more practical and realistic terms, this was no honeymoon any longer. This was a full-fledged family move with parents, children, and all their possessions traveling together!

I do remember in vivid terms the glorious arrival. And this time I had a wide view of the deck of the ship and the crowds on the pier awaiting, greeting, and waving to their loved ones, including our own family. Sharpest in my mind is the image of my mother's youngest brother who was athletic and proficient in gymnastics. He did not wait for our family's turn to descend the gangway. Instead, he somehow grabbed hold of the gangway ropes, and from the outside of the gangway, while people were descending; he lifted himself up to the deck. He was thus the first to greet us.

This is how my life began in Greece. There is one thing that prevailed: Despite my years of growing up there, deep inside me I always felt as an American. And this must have radiated, because often even some of my teachers addressed me as American—which was all right with me. Something prevailed that made my disposition uncommon or different from that of most other youngsters. Of course, I cannot attribute this to an environmental influence in the US—I was in Greece.

After all, I was only four years old when I was taken abroad. There was no possibility that environment had affected me. I have also stated that both my parents had been assimilated as Americans. I understand the impact this would have had upon me. My conviction is that this was not all. It goes without saying that environment exerts influence in the formation of character, habits, convictions, attitudes, and the like; and included is parental guidance and influence. Yet, in this case the influence of my parents at home was at par with that of my grandparents, uncles, aunts, and cousins with whom I was in constant and very close contact. In addition, there was also the unrelenting environment outside the home. To attribute it all to DNA is rather anemic as an explanation—our American way is just two hundred and forty years old; and many of us are very new here. After all, genes need more time to blend and to assert themselves. One might reason that, because others seemed to view me as American, I too began to be convinced. This too becomes debatable, when the question is asked: What made them see me as an American to start with?

There is no point in my belaboring this any longer. Suffice it to say that there was always a deep-rooted yearning in me to return home one day. I recall leafing through my father's American Legion magazines he received before the war. I often looked on the back cover of one that featured Mount Rushmore in an ad for Camel cigarettes. The artist had dramatized the image by giving it a reddish hue similar to the effect at sunset—more reminiscent of red soils are those of the Southwest; unlike the granite stones of Rushmore. My fond dream became to visit the site one day when back home. This was realized years later, after I visited all of the East Coast States and the rest of the mainland to the Pacific. Mount Rushmore was reserved as my last destination. Once this was accomplished, I knew I had come home. I should also add that in subsequent years I did not fail to visit Alaska and Hawaii as well. Furthermore, the case of the trip to Rushmore was for me a pending issue until it was fulfilled. It did not pose for me any demand to the exclusion of other travel or even residence abroad. It so happened that prior to Rushmore I did travel and did live abroad other than in Greece; and I do now continue to travel.

Life in Greece was normal for the family. The winters were spent in Athens and the summers in the mountains of Doris—the name defines the central part of Greece, and in general also known as Roumeli. These are, as I mentioned earlier, very ancient lands that were occupied by generations of migrants moving south and east from what was Illyria (area of Albania today).

My brother (right) and I in the mountains of Doris near
Mount Parnassus, during one of the pre-war summers.

The Aegean and Ionian cultures were created by the earlier migrants from the north who expanded eastward to the Aegean islands and to the coastal and eastern part of Asia Minor. Last to follow were the Dorians who brought along their own ethos and culture, and who were considered by their predecessors as brusque and undeveloped people. For anyone who is familiar in depth with the austere social principles and practices of these latter people; one can distinguish the traces even today. It includes the form of speech and enunciation when evaluated from a linguistic point of view. It came to pass that what was considered unrefined and backward, in time resulted in a stable and definitive part of classical civilization. A prominent and indisputable example of that is seen even today in the Doric style of architecture—the straightforward and somber simplicity of that form speaks for itself.

My life among such people was a rich source of personal development. This does not mean that somehow, I reveled in a sort of a superior life. All of my youthful years were full of the same sentiments, experiences, and encounters as those of any other youth. The positive element I seek to express is that from early on and even to this day, I have always been able to draw upon solid and reliable references for self-guidance. And again, I emphasize that this did not exclude me from the frailties of ordinary human life. The essential message one can draw from this is the important role that culture has in the formation of individual life; which when multiplied reflects on the outcome of a society as a whole. Culture, therefore, and thus civilization is the plying on of layers of experience and development of prior generations for newer ones to have and to use and enjoy. To discard previous learning on the grounds that it is old and useless is a cardinal social error. The adage that history repeats itself is an accurate description of what happens when cultural wealth is trashed. The notion that a current generation is wiser in its own right and at the exclusion of prior wisdom is a fallacy. Persons and societies who entertain such behavior always suffer and will continue to suffer the repercussions. My understanding of this principle came to me early in life. I did not fail to enjoy association, sports, and friendships with my peers; yet, I also favored to be in the presence of older persons, aware of the fact that I was gaining from their wisdom and advice. My key inspiration for this was the ancient anecdote about the old man who needed to start a fire.

He asked a little girl to run out and bring him a burning cinder. The child came back with the burning cinder in the palm of her hand. To his surprise the cinder was resting on top of a layer of ashes. This caused him to declare, "I grow old always learning."

More often than not it is much easier to destroy than it is to create and to maintain. This holds true for civilizations as well. For any society that demolishes or erases its past it is an irreplaceable loss with long-term effects to the detriment of its future generations. In a similar way, individuals reserve an advantage to themselves when they remain conscious of their own past, whether negative or positive. Reference to bygone experiences or to a general impression of lessons learned is a dependable compass for individuals to navigate in familiar and unfamiliar behavioral waters. A youthful generation stripped of this practice is destined to a future of unnecessary errors and suffering in an inevitable cycle of trying to rise again. All of the above is not to say that one should live life in the past. The opposite is intended. The past should only be used or exploited as a reference toward present and future advantage.

Were the standards mentioned a part of a four-year-old child's life? Of course not: such things took time to develop. As with any other youth, the environment along with parental guidance and that of other senior relatives laid the foundation for my general development. School, without question, held a preeminent importance in the process. I must say that even as a young child my concentration leaned more toward the abstract. It may be difficult to explain this. Yet, in spite of my appearance of drifting off away from the teachers' demand for full concentration, I still absorbed and retained information the same as my classmates. The issue presented more of a concern for my parents in the very early school years. Nevertheless, my progression carried on in normal fashion, even in the very strict setting of the Greek school system. The problem of schooling became one for every youth in Greece later when the Nazi and Fascist occupation took place. That period formed the critical time in very real terms that determined whether one had a genuine desire to focus and to learn.

THE SOUNDS OF WAR

I WAS NEAR FOURTEEN years old when the famous *No* was pronounced by the then Prime Minister of Greece, Ioannis Metaxas, to the ill-conceived demand of Benito Mussolini—which was for Greece to submit to his Mediterranean Basin (Mare Nostrum) fantasy of a no less ridiculous empire. Ridiculous as it was, the move also caused unprecedented misery, suffering, and loss of life and property. The whole nation of Greece fell into utter turmoil. Among the many disorders and disasters that plagued the country, formal schooling was one of the major victims. The teacher organizational system collapsed. Teachers the same as all other citizens faced terrible personal survival problems affecting them and their families. They too had to cope with the serious issues of lack of food (to a great degree in Athens); with salary problems due to progressive and unmanageable inflation; personal security problems in their homes and in the streets; the demands for resistance activities against the occupiers, whereby they joined by their own volition or were compelled to do so; the taking over of school facilities by the invaders to house their troops, and even burning school benches and the like to keep warm in the winter; and many other conditions that made survival or order untenable and at times even fatal.

My recommendation is for anyone interested in knowing the details of that period in Greece to read the book titled, *Inside Hitler's Greece, The Experience of Occupation, 1941-44*, by Mark Mazower, (1963), Yale University Press, New Haven and London (ISBN

0-300-06552-3 [pbk]). The work is an excellent account of events as they happened; except for one issue, in my opinion, that I will touch upon at a later time. Meanwhile, my goal is to continue my description of personal experiences during that particular period with as much accuracy as I can (I am writing this by memory, while closing in on my ninetieth year). This after all, is a personal anecdotal account rather than a scientific one. It is bent on conveying principles and emotional reflections as they affected my person. It is hoped that such will have a constructive impact on our millennial and upcoming generations.

It is more realistic in my own view that many folks, if not all, when going through times of danger not to recognize the full extent of their involvement. Yes, fear is often in play; but not awareness of certain dangers. From my own repeated experiences—as it may also occur with others—it is only after the situation is over that I begin to reflect on details and recognize the depth of what could have happened. In other instances, of course, when damage is already done, delayed reaction is different. It appears that during critical periods the human mind adapts to the situation, perhaps because of instinctive refuge to optimism; or perhaps due to the inability to process all of the circumstances involved. I believe that heroic actions come under this category. Often persons who have performed acts of heroism are unable or reluctant to ascribe to themselves precise reasoning for their actions. It is remarkable overall how adaptable the human mind is. Examples of this are the ability to adjust to hunger, tolerance in accepting abject living conditions, the continual sight of death during war time, and all such. Of course, the reverse is also true when favored by opulence and good fortune. People take for granted their good situation and at times without regard for others in need. The point here is that, granted the constant desire to be free of adversity, life during the years of occupation and its expected continuance had become the accepted mode of existence. What else could one do? In a progressive way, this type of tolerance erodes the finer nature of human beings. It is for this very reason that I stressed the importance of keeping high standards of civilized thinking as a refuge for a continued well-balanced life, even at times of adversity.

The date was 28 October 1940. That morning, I had just walked out the front door of our home on my way to school. I was attending the equivalent of Middle School at that time. For some reason I cannot recall, I had transferred from another school very near our home to one closer to downtown. It was the Third Gymnasium for Boys located in the Kolonaki section of Athens (Gymnasium in that system is Middle and High School). This required that I travel to school and back by streetcar, which I boarded at the main station close to home. The Station was the final or turnaround depot for the trip to the center of Athens. Often, I would cover the distance on foot as well.

I was in the middle of the street ready to reach the sidewalk across when the loudest morbid wailing sound of a siren began. This was a sudden and unfamiliar event for the citizenry; at least for that quiet and peaceful residential part of town. Even the existence of the siren was a novelty—a typical conic-shaped megaphone mounted on a black-colored metal frame on a rooftop nearby. All eyes turned toward the siren, being the source of that uncommon but compelling sound. Quick to learn afterwards was that the winding up-and-down tone meant alarm; while the continuous even-toned wail gave the all-clear. Just as quick was the understanding that the country was at war. Within a few hours the evidence became very clear. The elementary school located near our home was at once transformed. It was converted into a military conscription center, and instead of children being present, many men began to pour in and out, half-dressed in military clothing or carrying bundles of it as they left. The activity was frantic. Two of my mother's brothers reported there. The story is well-known. The comical Benito Mussolini (I beg latitude from my readers for my reference to him in this way. I always laugh when I see his theatrical poses and that face he would put on—and to think that people were impressed by that sort of thing!) had decided that the Mediterranean was all his property. He had developed visions of a new Roman empire that he would rule. To his misfortune, he proved to be a total failure. Prior to his aggression against Greece, he had launched an asymmetrical military attack against the far less prepared and equipped Ethiopian military. He had scored a temporary victory, but soon the tables were turned on him. His hallmark became defeat after defeat in his North African campaign.

His ultimatum against Greece demanding capitulation had the same fate. This was when the famous *No* response was given to him by the Greek leader, and when the two nations were at war.

There was justifiable pride in the Greek population concerning the performance of the military and the attitude of the citizenry when the Fascist attack occurred. The opening days of the conflict were alarming. The invaders were able to penetrate near one third of Greek territory. Soon afterwards things changed and the attackers were routed back deep into Albanian space from where they had come. There was heroism in the Greek military, including in the Greek women who played their critical role (even wading in ice cold rivers, lined up to pass supplies across). Once the Greek side recovered, the morale of the population rose. Despite the constant barrage of grim news coming from the front about the sacrifices of the military and the civilian population, the mood in the country had changed. Greek humor is often very subtle, scathing and seething— and not less philosophical. Derision of the Italian military was unforgiving. Mussolini, of course, had become the chief object of laughter in countless versions of art, music, lyrics, and prose. Even the Nazis, after entering Greece, picked up on the Greek style. And risking the alliance with the Italians, the Germans started to mock the Italians in the presence of the Greeks. It was very humiliating. I also recall the practice of marching the prisoners of war in the streets of the city—I don't know whether it was to relocate them or to parade them—and how the civilian population stood by in utter silence observing them. To some degree, there was an expression of near bewilderment in the people, trying to reconcile their emotions between hatred, pity, and delight. It was an internal human struggle to remain civilized. The marchers were human beings pacing down the road, stripped of their dignity—in unbuttoned uniforms, without their weapons, in a massive smell of disinfectant. I believe the bewilderment was the cause of the total silence.

There was good reason for authentic pride in those times. It was present even after the surrender that took place in Athens and during the occupation. My maternal grandfather one day was somewhere downtown, early during the occupation, walking with his son (the one who climbed the gangway and who was one of the conscripts when the war started). He, the son, had served at the Albanian front with the rank of sergeant. In the aftermath of the hostilities and with the disarray that followed, he along with many other soldiers was forced to walk home all the way from the front. My grandfather and he were taken by surprise when a stranger ran up to them and in great excitement told my grandfather that he recognized my uncle as the first soldier to have walked into the city of Argyrokastron when it was liberated from the Fascists during the Italian retreat.

The Albanian war was not the only plague that struck the Greek nation at one and the same time. A second front was created at the Bulgarian border with Greece. The reason for that conflict is well known. I will touch on it in brief in order to establish a foundation for the rest of what is to be described ahead.

For some reason, the era of the second quarter of the twentieth century seems to have been a sprouting season for dangerous megalomaniacs such as the infamous Benito Mussolini, Joseph Stalin, Adolf Hitler, Francisco Franco, Juan Peron, Josip Broz Tito, Mao Tse-Tung, Hirohito of Japan, and to a lesser degree even Ioannis Metaxas, etc. I bring up Metaxas, because at first he was an admirer of Mussolini and his methods. He had a change of mind when reality set in and his country was challenged by the latter. In my view, Metaxas over-extended himself trying to reshape his society. For example, he attempted a youth organization that lacked the basic leadership before he could even dream of its final success. In other words, he had not first organized and trained the basic leadership cadre that was needed before mobilizing the masses of students. I estimate that at that time I was in early Middle School. All that Metaxas came up with was to have a whole number of students dressed up in blue and white uniforms with caps. No teachers were prepared for that type of organization. On one occasion, all the schools gathered at the Pedion Areos (Mars Square), a spacious public park near the Military Academy, where Metaxas as leader was scheduled to appear. Up to a point the teachers were able to maintain normal control of their students; and had instructed them to show an enthusiastic greeting when their chief leader would appear. The children took the instruction with much seriousness. All was fine up to that point. When Metaxas appeared, the pent-up anticipation of the children broke out and the result was unbelievable. Amid cheers and loud screaming, the children in one sudden outburst all stormed toward Metaxas to greet him. I was placed in the front lines and I had to run. It was chaos. Metaxas started to call out over the loud-speaker for the children to go back; and he even walked out toward them with outstretched arms and open palms to push them back—as though it were possible. I bring this up, because the student he touched in the chest with both palms, out of all those thousands, was I (a curious omen of the time, that without slipping away from the subject, I would like to mention: It seems that by the touch of that man—not as a person, but as head of state—in the years that followed after the war and all, I kept bumping into presidents and heads of state in the US and abroad. I was never in politics, so it was either casual or in non-political settings). Later, things started to slow down, and soon the crowd dispersed. Another admirer of Mussolini was Hitler. In this instance, the change of mind for Hitler when reality set in was for himself to become even worse than his idol—that instead of opposing he was forced to assist. The two allies of Nazi Germany were Fascist Italy and Imperial Japan. Of the two, it would appear that only Japan stood up in Hitler's esteem (although later defeated by the Americans). Italy was an embarrassment to Hitler. The Albanian campaign against Greece was a clear and final indicator of Italy's negative contribution to the said Axis tripartite union. It is worthy to note that the success of the Albanian campaign was the first victory to be scored against the Axis in World War II. Prime Minister Winston Churchill made the effort to inspire Allied resistance by pronouncing words such as, it should not be said that Greeks fight like heroes, but that heroes fight as the Greeks do. To be sure, this type of eloquence was inspiring. Yet, the onslaught of two military forces against a smaller power could not block Hitler's advancement; even with British participation on mainland Greece and in Crete where another defensive campaign was waged—the Allied forces had withdrawn to that island after the mainland was lost. We have seen that the Italian forces experienced repeated losses in Africa. Yet, Hitler had been inspired by the ambitions of Mussolini and his Mare Nostrum etc. He expanded his outlook for a larger Germany by including Romania and the oil supplies there. The Caucuses were not far from his thinking either, and the oil resources in that region. He expected that Italy would penetrate Greek space in favor of the Axis and set the stage for an expansion in Africa. Everything was delayed and Hitler was forced to take on an active role in the Balkans in order to rescue the Italians and to advance into Greece himself. He attacked Greece at the Bulgarian border and established a second front for the Greeks. To his surprise, he too got bogged down for a period of three weeks with many losses and unable to penetrate the Greek defenses— namely, the Rupel Line. What glorious days were those for the Greeks! The great conqueror and strategist got stuck! And like the Persians of old at Thermopylae, the only way he was able to succeed was to invade Greece from the Yugoslavian side and neutralize the Greek defenders from the rear. A disgrace for Hitler! By the way, Yugoslavia (west of Bulgaria) and Greece maintained good relations and defenses there offered softer conditions for the Germans to enter Greece. Another reason German forces focused on the Greek border west of Bulgaria was their attempt to join up with the Italians in Albania. The retreat to the island of Crete followed and the point of defense was established there. The Germans for the first-time in that engagement used paratroopers to invade the island. Victory was achieved, but at such a high cost that never again did they attempt such an operation. The final strategic retreat of the Allied forces was to Africa.

Souda Bay, Crete where the German paratroopers met with their ultimate destruction as an effective military unit—never used again in WWII. The left photograph shows the Allied cemetery of the fallen in battle. The German cemetery is on the right. The background of each photograph shows the Bay. The drop zone where the battle took place appears between the cemetery and the water in the photograph on the right.

At this point, I would like to digress for a few moments to mention the Rupel defense line and Mount Athos. Some years ago in one of our trips to Greece with my wife, among other sectors we also drove to the northern parts. It was a long-held wish of mine to visit and have a personal acquaintance with the Rupel fortification. This was for me a deep desire, because of the solemnity of the sacrifices that took place there, and for the historic significance in demolishing Hitler's arrogance. Besides that, we had a family member who had fought in Albania and had received a head wound. He was sent back to Athens to recover and before long was rushed to Rupel to fight as a machine gunner. He survived. Rupel is an underground fortification on the border between Greece and Bulgaria. The entrance to Rupel is controlled and tours are scheduled on special times. My entry was denied. Time was limited for us and there was no way we could wait. We drove down the slopes to the nearest town at the military installation where also the command is for the fort. I walked up to the sentry and petitioned to talk to the officer in charge. It was not granted, but I was asked to explain my request. The sentry was sensitive to my plea and must have conveyed the right description to his commander—not due to my foreign appearance, clothing, etc., but the fluency of my Greek must have convinced them that I could go. Permission was granted and we returned to the guardhouse. My wife was accommodated in a waiting area and I was escorted into the installation by a soldier. It was an emotional experience to walk through a good portion of the fort and even to climb up the rungs of the narrow dugout to the machine gun nest up top. The narrow slit offered a wide-angle view of the descending slopes that the gunner could see and control. Small wonder the Germans failed to penetrate the line. Besides the underground defenses, the Greek forces had also neutralized the rushing river nearby. They embedded inclined logs in the river-bottom facing the current. To avoid the fortified positions, when the Germans floated downriver in their rafts, they were always destroyed by those embedded poles. There was also a larger general-view installation that I visited. The soldier told me that often old-timers arriving at that point would break down and begin to shed tears. As he spoke and turned to look at me, I saw his expression that he had no need to say more. In a truest sense, I share with all our American veterans the same sentiment about Europe, Asia-Pacific, Middle-East, Africa, and all other times and places.

We left Rupel and in a short time we were at Ouranoupolis. Distances in Greece are quite short. When reading road maps, drivers should be prepared not to overshoot their destinations. Also, be careful of curves and up-and-down roads: there are many and they come up quick. Ouranoupolis means, "Heaven City." It is located at the border of Mount Athos, the mountainous peninsula of the monastic enclosure of the Greek Orthodox faith. On the way, south to Ouranoupolis, not detectable unless one looks for it, there is a ditch that one crosses. It looks as if of no consequence because it is an ordinary ditch with weeds growing inside. It has a historical past, being the ditch Xerxes ordered dug through the peninsula to slide his ships across. He did this to avoid navigating around the peninsula and to save time. We decided that I would make a brief entry to Mount Athos. To start with, entry there is not simple. Advanced arrangements are required and often can take months. I am not certain whether non-Orthodox folks can enter. The fact is that the monks are adamant (and I did hear it when inside) that the entry there is not for the purpose of tourism. Scheduling and conforming to requirements is how to obtain entrance permission. Access is never by land, because no one crosses the northern border of the mountainous enclave. The only access is by sea, boarding at Ouranoupolis and landing at the coast near the monasteries. There is an office in the town where these arrangements are made for entry permission and to obtain boarding passes on the vessel.

There is much and rich history concerning the twenty monasteries there. And do not believe for a moment that these are petty structures. The monasteries are gigantic stone-built structures that have lasted for centuries, and which have often been defended in quasi-military manner by the monks. The Byzantine emperors had a strong hand in the founding of these religious establishments. The structures have been erected on various sites of the peninsula, either low at the coastal foot of the rugged mountains or high on the rocky and inaccessible slopes. The views of them and from them are not easy to describe with words, considering the breathtaking terrain features and the surrounding blue waters. Once a person enters that environment, the psychological impact is unquestionable. There is a definite sacredness that overtakes a person due not only to the suggestiveness of the environment, but to the authentic purity that prevails. It is for this elevated state of existence (not physical wealth and advantage) that monasticism is pursued. And those who enter that environment, even for a brief period, become affected. It was clear to me how changed the surrounding atmosphere was among my travel companions on the return trip aboard the ship.

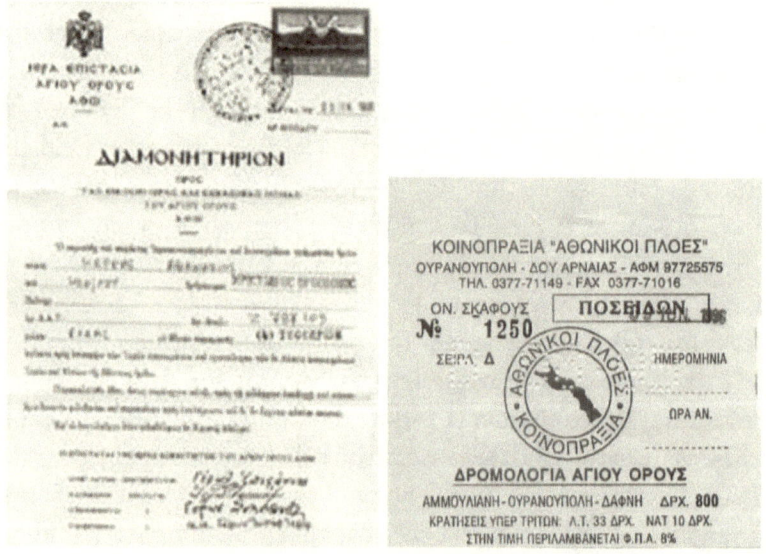

(Left) Admission document to Mount Athos.
(Right) Boarding pass to sail to Mount Athos.

The overall delay experienced in Greece, caused Hitler's plan against the Soviet Union to be thwarted. His defeat in Russia was because he got trapped by the severe winter weather without adequate preparation. Two reasons are given for his delay to start the Russian campaign. One is that he was unable to move any earlier than June due to the preceding heavy rains and the muddy and impassable conditions that were created.

The campaign had to be postponed until the grounds were dry. The second reason is the one already explained as it relates to the delay caused by the Greek campaign.

The first reason is of course logical and acceptable, but with an exception: The second reason is indisputable. It seems that any strategist planning a major assault against a vast territory where timing is of extreme importance on account of severe weather, would never dilute the attacking force by shipping parts of it off to another distant operation whose outcome could not be assured. It would also appear that an impending serious campaign such as that against Russia would not only have demanded the presence of the entire complement of troops, but also a readiness to move at a moment's notice. This did not appear to have been the case at the Russian front when a major body of the force was otherwise diverted and entangled in a series of decisive battles in the Balkans far away from Russia. In addition, it is evident that the paratrooper unit dropped in Crete must have been held in highest esteem by the Germans as an effective assault unit. It could have been used in a very practical way by dropping behind the Russian lines past the wet lands—the Soviets too would have been pinned down in the wetlands the same as the Germans. Instead we find that the paratrooper unit was just wasted in Crete and never used again. It is clear that the attention of Hitler was divided. He had to be in too many places at the same time. The failures of Mussolini in Africa and in Greece caused Hitler the loss of the war in Russia. His delay to start the Russian campaign and the winter weather that soon followed formed the beginning of his destruction. Hitler should not have admired Mussolini so much.

Nor Metaxas in Greece should have emulated his Fascist counterpart; although the Italian attack would have come anyway, regardless whether Greece had a dictator. The war went on. The excitement of victory soon was replaced by a mood of anxiety, sadness, fear, and doubt. It was impossible for the Greek defenses to hold any longer. A small non-industrial nation fighting with bare hands against heavy weaponry and mechanized armor had but one destiny only. The first to roll into Athens were the Germans. They had first dibs on everything. After all, they were the accomplished victors. The Germans knew it, the Greeks knew it, and the Italians knew it. The question in the minds of the people was how the Germans will behave. Do not be misled. It turns out that although the Italians on some nebulous and ineffective occasions reverted to their Mediterranean nature of affinity toward their neighbor; they displayed their own utter savagery and criminality. They had become ugly as occupiers on various occasions. At the command level, it is reported they displayed instances for a fairer treatment of the population. The general perception concerning the Germans was that they were cold, remote, and fear-producing. My say is, occupiers or not, they did not belong there. Their presence in a land of and among a people over whom they had no claim or earned cultural credit, they were a disgrace to the human race and unto themselves. The sight of them at the Acropolis next to the Parthenon was repugnant, off balance, and uncivilized. The swastika; flying on the Acropolis? What connection is there? Think about it! Only a barbarian usurper would contemplate such an act.

It is as simple as that. Needless to say, that atrocities committed by both invading groups will remain as black marks in the annals of true history, both written and unwritten.

OCCUPATION BEGINS

THE DATE WAS 27 April 1941. That time of the year is when the weather in Attica is beautiful. The sun shines and the red poppies bloom in all the fields with breathtaking effect. A number of people were gathered at the intersection of the Kifissias and Alexandras Boulevards. This was the location of the streetcar turnaround terminal for the ride toward the city center—the Omonia, or Concord. The section of the city is known as Ampelokipi (or Vinegardens). It was then, and now it continues to be a main intersection. It is situated on the route that Marathon runners follow on their way to the finish line at the old pure white-marble National Stadium. Ampelokipi was the location where the surrender of Athens took place. I will take a moment to describe the city layout in that area for a better understanding of my upcoming references. The description is simple: Kifissias Boulevard runs north and south, and Alexandras Boulevard runs east and west. Their crossing is located at the east end of Alexandras. And at that east end, Alexandras extends past Kifissias and is named Fidipidou. Many references will be made to Alexandras, as it divides the area of Ampelokipi into north and south sections. This was the area where I grew up and I knew every inch of it. Much of that area, if not everything, has stayed the same to this day. I have returned there several times and can still identify details etched in my memory since boyhood. There are sidewalk tiles, for example, that I still recognize when I pace over them, the same as I did seventy-seven years ago on my way to school. Considering the years that have lapsed, this at a minimum testifies to the excellent building skills and methods of the old artisans. My knowledge of the neighborhood, of course, also included knowledge of the neighbors. And that day I knew who stood by around me in my specific vicinity when the surrender was signed. I did not witness the proceedings as such, because that happened in a restaurant on Fidipidou, around the corner from where I was. I stood with other inquisitive onlookers in the middle of the pavement on the deserted Kifissias. That was in front of what today is a French-chain-supermarket. In those years only empty lots were there. The Germans had backed up and parked two open-top military personnel vehicles in the space that today is a sidewalk across from the said supermarket. My brother was also among the bystanders. We had gone there together. I can claim then, that in that group of people in that vicinity, and to the extent that I could observe, only two American-born citizens witnessed what was going on—namely, my brother and me. For some reason, one of the Germans urged me to approach and sit in one of those two vehicles. A refusal would have been awkward if not risky, not knowing what their reaction would be for me and others around. No smiles were in play. My explanation to this day is that the German was trying to "play nice" in the presence of the public (if so, that is not at all what happened in the country in the dismal years that followed). In any event, I was on that thing for a few moments, when for some reason my mother's oldest brother happened to come by (perhaps also to witness) and when he saw me he gave me an eye-piercing nod to come off the vehicle. The Germans saw him but did not object—maybe to keep looking "nice." It was my chance to climb out, and I did. I bring up the incident, because in Mazower's book those first two personnel vehicles to enter Athens are seen in a photograph on page five proceeding down town. I sat in one of them. They appear traveling toward Constitution Square (Syntagma) where Vassilissis Sofias Boulevard ends. And the streetcar rails seen on that boulevard are those on which I traveled to go to school.

This first day was the mold that set the course for the occupation of Greece. Suffering, hunger, killing, deprivation, confusion, were but few of the experiences that befell the country. To some degree everyone became a victim—some more some less, but none escaped. It fostered the ability to adapt to the conditions. As mentioned earlier, there is an innate human aptitude to do this, and even to get adjusted to it. Yet, most will struggle with the desire to extricate themselves. In general, those who find comfort in continuing are those who prefer or who manage to convert adversity to their advantage or profit; and often to do so at the expense of others. Such reactions may be chalked up as weakness, necessity, bad judgment, ideology, and even the conscious willingness to do so by exploiting, cheating, and extorting. The most repugnant reason, of course, is the last. When social upheavals happen, as for example, war, occupation, general disorder, and the like; that is the time when the fabric of civility comes unraveled. The threshold of propriety drops and people become licentious and indifferent to communal integrity. The same effect takes place when the quality of political leadership deteriorates. It is inevitable that large societies are formed by entrusting order and their governance to central powers. This occurs because it is not possible for single individuals to handle more than their own immediate environment and issues. As a consequence, they are forced to delegate many decisions and obligations to some type of central care or authority. The key is to be able to harness such representative authority, so it does not overpower the very source that places it there—that source being the individual members. In the case of the invasion and occupation of Greece, two concurrent events took place: One was the collapse of the organizational integrity of the society. That is, no Greek government authority existed that was respected by all quarters and with a say-so over the Germans. And second, the German authority that was established was not accountable to or under the control of the people. In other words, the population in terms of families or persons, was left to fend on its own. All the Nazis cared about was to rob the food production of Greece and to send it to their own; and to control the population, in order to be able to continue the first thing and for their military strategic purposes. Their regard for human life was downgraded in progressive fashion the longer they stayed in the country.

The result of all the above was devastation. This was more severe in the city of Athens; because in the country, the people were able to garner food from their lands. There were, of course, great atrocities committed in the open country in the smaller settlements by both occupiers whenever they acted on reprisals against the resistance. The issue of hunger in Athens reached unspeakable levels causing the death of tens of thousands. I was often witness to truckloads of fresh vegetables and fruits being carted north on Vassilissis Sofias Boulevard (while I was suffering lack of food myself). It was heart-rending to witness a man walking in the middle of the street through the neighborhoods with a little boy he held by the hand. As he walked he would cry out: "We are hungry my ladies, we are hungry." The child was as a little ghost, thin and pale, with rags for clothes as was he, and no expression in his innocent eyes. The man, as I recall while I write this, was bloated up from head to toe and his skin was purple blue. This is the truth, and I defer to any MD right now to tell me how a human being in that shape can still be able to walk down the street and even put out a pleading cry for help. No one helped him. No one had anything to give him. And if they did, they kept it for themselves. As I said, it is uncanny how well the human can adapt to circumstances, and even become heartless. (So, don't talk to me about Nazis, Fascists, Communists, Capitalists, Theists, Atheists, Meat-eaters, and Vegetarians. I know about it. Unless you feel for others what you feel for yourself, the only one you love is you).

Many instances can be given about the issue of food shortages in Athens. It was not an economic issue that often produced the inability to find food. The problem was the inability to find the source that could satisfy the need. The black market was rampant in Athens. For most people, the practice was not considered acceptable, and black marketers were beneath public esteem. Often their greed exceeded the limits. Public need almost seemed to justify their existence, and things got pretty serious. Individuals who engaged in excessive practice just for their own enrichment at the expense of their fellow citizens were worthy of full public contempt. This contempt today should not only extend to the perpetrators themselves, whether they remained in Greece or emigrated abroad, but also to their offspring: because they are living off of blood money. Only those who lived through that dreadful period and who know and understand what happened, are able to express an opinion on the matter. I was more than fascinated once, when two presumed intellectuals laughed at the subject in admiration of wealth gotten that way—typical of a cultural view empty of human value. Their scornful dismissal made them repugnant and little as human beings. But, of course, they didn't fancy themselves that way. I repeat: How can it be otherwise from someone who has not gone through a similar ordeal?

Bakeries that existed in Athens before the war remained active during the occupation. This was true for many other businesses at the outset of the occupation. The main difference was whether all of them were able to remain productive and useful to the public. A more accurate description of reality is to say that businesses as well as individual persons all became anemic and less vibrant with time. How can an economy prosper when trade, both domestic and foreign, comes to a dead still? How can commerce move, when within the country activity in goods, services, and people is blocked? How can the population feel vibrant and invigorated when their mobility is controlled or prohibited? In other words, the framework of society at first remained in place, but the ability to function was curtailed. With time, due to that inertia and the increasing food shortages, other essential needs, and inflation, the economic system was in shambles.

Confusion set in. Although some bakeries may have stayed in place (a basic need for life), other components and functions of the economy soon began to erode and disappear. The professions such as teachers, lawyers, doctors, engineers, many began to be displaced. The order of the day was how to make the next deal for survival, regardless of one's profession or status. When it came to food, there was little that dignity could offer. Those with street smarts had a better chance to survive. So much of this happened, that even after liberation, the cultural framework of the society had changed forever. There was no turning back to the old ways. Everyone had become underprivileged, and when recovery began, the more competent, or more audacious, or more pragmatic ones were winning the day. Many of the rich, of course, stayed rich, and many of the nouveau riche likewise. Some had interacted if not collaborated with the occupiers for reasons of survival, and others because they were weak, unprincipled, or traitors.

Anyway, as things became harder for the occupiers, they also got harder for the vanquished. The rations for bread became scantier, and the substance that they were supposed to entitle the holder to became even worse. At first, the amount of bread one received started to diminish and got smaller and smaller. Coupons representing rations were issued. Soon, the quality of the bread deteriorated. And later, there was no quality of bread whatsoever. The substance doled out was from some sort of seed that had no nutritional value, and the product had to be baked and served with paper in the bottom so it would not crumble. As for satisfying hunger pangs by eating that stuff, it was sheer sarcasm and a shame to stand in line to receive it. No doubt, that the black *marketeers* and traitors had a hand in this as well. Unless one was connected with such an element there was little that could be done. The issue, as I said, was not the money; although one could not function without it, as is the case everywhere. Yet, money alone could not always answer the need for a source of supply. Nonetheless, our family managed to survive. There were days that we came to a complete impasse. Other days we had to submit to difficulty. The overall experience was bleak. Any opportunity for finding food was a good opportunity. I do not remember how it happened, but on one occasion I had found out that there was a shepherd who had come down off the mountains and hills with his flock of sheep to graze them near Athens. It was a long-time practice for sheep and goat herders to do this in pursuit of greener pastures at lower elevations. The site I refer to was considered in the outskirts of Athens in those years. It was at a distance of some three and one-half miles from our home, which meant I walked about an hour in each direction to get to the pen. I forget what type of container I used. The point is, I would buy a certain quantity of fresh milk and bring it back home before the others woke up. The milk would be boiled and served at breakfast. The success of that mission is evident; which is to say, the praises I received exceeded my expectations. So, for that season the enterprise became a duty in my mind. I would awake at around four in the morning, begin my trip, and returned home by six-thirty. I would receive my deserved kudos and an authentic breakfast along with the rest of my family. Needless to say, that my mother was ecstatic about the whole thing, being able to dispense some authentic nourishment for the duration of that activity.

The shepherds were able to penetrate the space with their flocks because they arrived via open mountains and fields and avoided the roadway checkpoints controlled by the Nazis and the Fascists. At this point of my writing, I would like to add that I am only relating my own experiences and activities, and not those of my siblings. To do so would be an intrusion. To the contrary, my introduction of my parents and other references about them, is intended to honor and to memorialize them.

Mention made above about the shepherds and their grazing methods prompts me to digress again for a moment. I will describe a pre-war event that I enjoyed with one of my uncles. The rural connection of the family with the folk in the Doric mountains was never diminished. More than one of the shepherds who descended into Attica with their herds were from those environs and at times akin to us in Athens. This meant that we could visit them in the open where they were established for the season, and enjoy the richness of their lives as shepherds. Their possessions were not simple: Their shelter, bedding, apparel, utensils, and all other necessities were the finest for that type of life. These were people who almost year-round resided in open space. They moved about as families: young and old, healthy and good-looking, marrieds and new-borns, singles and in-laws, one coordinated unit, and with hundreds of animals. It was an experience I will not forget. The biggest treat for me was that my uncle had been invited to go because it was Easter time and they wanted him to join them. Well, Easter in Greece is the best season—not only because of the religious atmosphere that prevails, but also because little compares with Attica in the spring time. Above that, was the location the shepherds had chosen. It was the headlands on which Xerxes stood when far below he could watch with dismay and horror the destruction of his fleet by the Greek navy at the strait of Salamis. Well, I too saw the panorama—ships or no ships. The difference was that instead, I had enjoyed the weather, the company, the festivities, and the jubilation of Easter along with the same dramatic view!

Let's get back to the war. Not because I like it. It's because the critical years of my youthful life, when I started to know myself, were times that affected me in a very inordinate way. I believe this to be the same for any young person, when beyond their own will they are coerced to build their life under abnormal conditions. I am not alone in this. There are millions around the world who are or have been affected this way. I think of the young children who have yet to understand themselves who have to endure the doings of adults. What are their impressions of what life is about? At this point, I am only describing my own experience, so I will continue. Before I proceed, I will express praises for a young sixteen-year-old underground member, who caught up in the fervor of that period, did something most extraordinary to soothe the soul of every Greek person—but also to humiliate the arrogance of every Nazi. He climbed up on the Acropolis and managed to bring down the swastika flying at the chief and most eminent spot in Athens and all of Greece and abused it. He was arrested and tortured to such a degree that his health was affected for life. There isn't a person who has not admired him. That is Greece.

Food, of course, was not the only issue that impacted life. Clothing too was a problem. For example, one cannot wear the same pair of shoes forever and expect them to remain intact. This was more so in Athens where folks do a lot of walking—a lot even today. This is not for lack of transportation these days. The fact is that Athens has put in place a very modern and efficient subway system that in terms of service, noise, and esthetics is excellent. The way the city is sectioned, it is often inviting to walk rather than to ride. Unlike the long blocks existing in the east-west direction of streets in New York City, for example, the arrangement in Athens is far more manageable. Anyway, transportation in Athens was not paralyzed altogether in those times; yet, for sundry reasons mobility had subsided. Perhaps this was because of service interruptions, the inflationary effect, even the problem of less street exposure for security reasons. Life was slowed down. Unless one happened with adequate styles and changes of clothing from before the war, it did not appear that the population was going about in fancy wear. The mood overall had become somber. It always appeared to me that even when the sun was out, the sky overhead was a steady grey. And as I mentioned, there was the constant concern about personal security. It was always there. Anything could happen to anyone at any moment. And everyone would talk about it, until the next incident. It could be something that happened to me, or to a stranger, or to a relative or friend, that we heard about. It could be an incident of any sort. There was no lack of variety. One day, for example, my brother came home alarmed and in turmoil. His friend at school (whom I had also met many times) had been picked up by the Germans and taken to a room where they hung him up by his thumbs. I never learned what the outcome of that was. People were getting slapped around, kicked, and stabbed. There are at least three occasions that I can relate that happened to me. The fact I am here to write about them does not mean the incidents were simple or free of danger, compared to those where persons suffered physical damage or even death. It is not so. All incidents were fraught with danger for everyone. Some folks were lucky and did not get hurt, or imprisoned, or killed, while others had to endure such pains. Anything that may have started as a simple event, could have escalated to a catastrophe at any time. Conditions were always unpredictable. For example, whenever I went to school on foot, I had to pass the location where today is the US Embassy. Then, I had to walk the length in front of a military installation, which was there since before the war for the Greek army. The Italians had taken it over. On the occasion when they either raised or lowered their flag with the corresponding music, all civilians within sight or hearing had to stop and stand at attention. To me and everyone else among the Greek folk, their flag was spoken of as a dishrag—except that, for practical reasons we had to submit. Open defiance had no place there. That was the function of the organized underground resistance, not of the single individual who may or may not have been armed. The bitter sentiments, of course, were running very high as may well be imagined. At times, there were pedestrians going by, not regular users of the route. They did not know the rule and they did not stop. That, right there, became a major change in their life—a change in one moment to the next. Everyone was at risk. And there was no measure of the quality or amount of risk, or where an incident would end.

The US embassy in Greece had given notice for Americans to leave Greece. Meanwhile, the Atlantic Ocean had become a target for Hitler, attacking shipping to minimize or eliminate support coming across from America. The decision of my parents was to stay. Other Greek-Americans did likewise. Then, Greece fell and occupation began. The home that was given to my mother at her marriage was put up for sale, since the money source in the US was blocked. Also, outlandish inflation began to take its toll on the value of American notes payable after the war and exchanged for Greek currency—one hundred dollars today converted to Greek money was worth ten dollars tomorrow. The Nazis saw to that for the Greek economy. All they did was print Greek money without limit. This gave them the means to claim they were legitimate buyers of Greece's wealth—more in particular the country's agricultural or food production. In other words, they were criminals and murderers. Tens of thousands perished because of hunger. Today there are those who feel they don't owe anything to Greece for what their predecessors did. People often carted bags filled with paper money just to conduct simple transactions. I remember running a chore for my grandmother, and I brought back paper change in a bag. She took it mumbling a scornful remark, stuffed it in a small burner and set fire to it. She boiled water for an herb tea. Her action was one of indifference. She regarded it as waste paper. It was. Notice below how the denominations escalated. The result was that too many zeros didn't fit on the bills, and it was also hard to tell the difference. The problem was solved by just printing the number followed by a word instead of zeros. Following are images of bills issued under Nazi occupation during 1942-1944. Read down in the left column and then the right, first in the upper and then in the lower section. Inflation spiraled up and became massive in 1944. The value in the last bill listed below would not have bought more than a streetcar fare for two. The currency is in Drachmas:

Drachmas: 1,000 – 5,000 – 10,000 – 25,000 – 50,000 – 100,000

Drachmas: 500,000 – 1,000,000 – 5,000,000 – 10Million – 25Million – 500Million – 2,000Million

The need arose for my parents to rent a place for our new home. Years prior, an Englishman in Athens had built a very nice residence in the vicinity where our own home was. The property had come into the possession of a well-to-do Greek gentleman. It was in effect an estate with a villa, having three stories and a single-story wing, a surrounding garden, a stone-wall and iron fence, a heavy front-entrance iron gate, and a circular driveway. Our family occupied the second and third floors, while the first floor was occupied by the French chargé d'affaires in Athens and his family (Mazower's book mentions the said diplomat on page two hundred and forty-five, referring to the diplomat's efforts for the Nazis to ease up on the Jewish people). It happens that the French family had engaged a lady teacher of English for their three children. It was a unique opportunity for us to obtain the teacher's valuable service for my siblings and myself. In the process, my father and the teacher began conversations in French and often exchanged views about the progress of the war. Some time later, the said diplomat was transferred, but my father remained in touch with the teacher who was still in Athens. By some means, that lady was receiving newspapers from France. I do not know whether they were from the established press under the Germans or the underground. Whatever it was, one evening my father asked me to go to the teacher's home and bring back some of the issues she promised him. He also cautioned me to be careful. Lo and behold on my return that night, as I neared our place, I was able to discern a group of four or five Italians coming toward me. It was quite dark. I knew they were Italians, because they were boisterous and loud in their language. My thought was to drop the papers. Yet, I feared that they would be able to see something white falling from my hand or that they would hear something fall. I did nothing and kept walking. Then, that's all I remember. I do not know what they did with me. One thing was obvious that at least they had hit me, but to what extent I don't know, because I had blacked out. When I came to, my nose was bleeding and running down my chest, it was a sudden waking, the papers were still clinched in my hand, and that gang had gone. I couldn't hear their voices any longer. I gathered my wits and continued home. It was a piece of good fortune for me, because who knows what would have happened, had they noticed the newspapers and began to investigate. Leaflet distribution and printed propaganda was a very big no-no by both Germans and Italians. Also, no open radios were permitted. All radios had to be modified only to receive the local Athens broadcasts controlled by the Nazis or the Fascists. No overseas reception was allowed, and that is why my father was eager to get those French newspapers in order to find out something about what was going on in the world. I mentioned earlier that other Greek-Americans had remained in Greece the same as our family did. The early victories in Albania contributed to a sense of assurance if not euphoria. As time marched on before Greece's fall, it all began to change: Elation became sadness; rejoicing became cries; assurance became doubt; and so on. The presence of Allied troops along with the Greek forces prior to the fall was a welcome sight. Yet, the screeching Stukas dive-bombers blasting the port of Piraeus had the opposite effect. And, while I am on that subject, let me mention that one of the targets the Germans hit must have been a ship carrying Turkish paper currency. The explosion was very powerful. It jettisoned the paper money high and wide into the atmosphere. And thousands of bills in the air traversed the city of Athens and came from the port clear across to Ampelokipi and rained down upon us. I had picked up several of them. Below is an image of one of those bills.

Turkish currency blown in the air by a Stukas bombing raid
at the port of Piraeus against ships docked there.

British, Australian, New Zealand, and Indian troops were all in Greece. Soon, the breakdown happened and everything disappeared. A morbid silence and the grey skies took over. Kindness was substituted by harshness and brutality. It was not just the Jews in Salonika (Thessaloniki) who suffered (and they did in major ways)—it was all of Greece. By the way, many Jewish people were sheltered by Greek families during that ordeal. My oldest son's godfather, a furrier by profession, was one of those who helped. He related this to me years later in Santiago, Chile where he had his business and where my wife and I and our children resided for a few years. He told me that there were several cases like that. Salonika, of course, was a major Jewish population center, where years prior a great number had migrated from Spain to escape persecution. Germans found fertile ground in that city for their distorted obsession. Somehow, in subtle ways, people began to be for themselves only. They had to. It was a form of defense against the reality of having to cope with pain. They became hard. Survival was the order of the day. In one instance toward the end of occupation, a new matter showed up. As I said, anything could happen at any moment without reason. The announcement was made that all Americans (at least in Athens that I know about) must report to the Kommandantur and must bring along all their credentials such as passports, etc. To this day, some seventy-two years later, I still haven't the slightest idea what this was for. Only two possibilities come to my mind: one is that they wanted us as hostages, since they anticipated losing and they needed a negotiating tool with the Americans; or, number two, they wanted to weed out any Jewish-Americans who may have been among us, so they could finish their dirty work. There is one remaining possibility that US pressure sought and obtained protection for American citizens under Swiss neutrality. Yet as we shall see, this does not hold up well, considering what happened to our documents. The outcome for us was that we were never arrested or kept, and we never heard from them again. Yet, we did come under one action: We appeared as ordered at the assigned location with all our documents (in our case, with our US passports). The site they had selected was a downtown basement-theater lobby. The arrangement of the place was two separate descending marble staircases from the street entrance to the ticket lobby below. I remember we were outside lined up on the sidewalk on the right side as we faced the building. It was cloudy and rainy and I felt cold, even though it was summer.

We descended the right-side stairway and on arrival we faced a table in the middle of the lobby. There was a person sitting behind the table who took our documents. A couple of others stood by. One was a tall grey or white-headed man from the Swiss Consulate in Athens. And without fail standing by, there was the good old Nazi with the gun at the ready. The result: Our passports were taken and we never saw them again. Instead a substitute single-page letter was given to each of us—headed by the Department for the Protection of Foreign Affairs of the Swiss Consulate in Athens and printed on one side in German and the other in Greek. It identified us as American citizens under protection. I still have it. It was the only document we could later present to the US Consular authorities in Greece for recovering our identity and returning to the States. Who knows what the Germans were intending? The truth is that there was great confusion and anxiety about it all. For them, we would have served as instruments for negotiation, and not because they loved us. The bottom line is that they departed Greece without fighting. And, the reason for that is that they scurried out of Greece, only to escape being cut off by the Russians in the Balkans. In any event, it was an ominous message to go down the right side stairway as American citizens, and to come up the left side as *protected* American citizens.

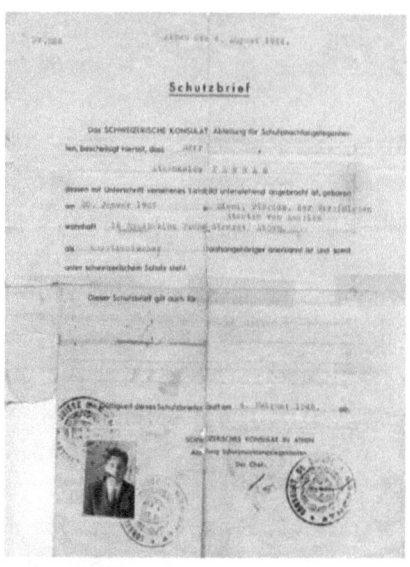

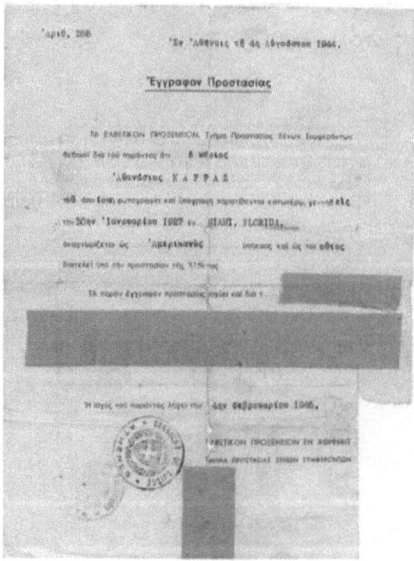

Above are copies of a single two-sided document received in lieu of my American passport taken by the Germans. The front side is in German and the reverse is in Greek. (The brown strips are ordinary tape to keep the paper together). Letter was dated 4 August 1944 and was invalid after 4 February 1945. Athens was free by 12 October, 1944. Greece overall was free by May 1945.

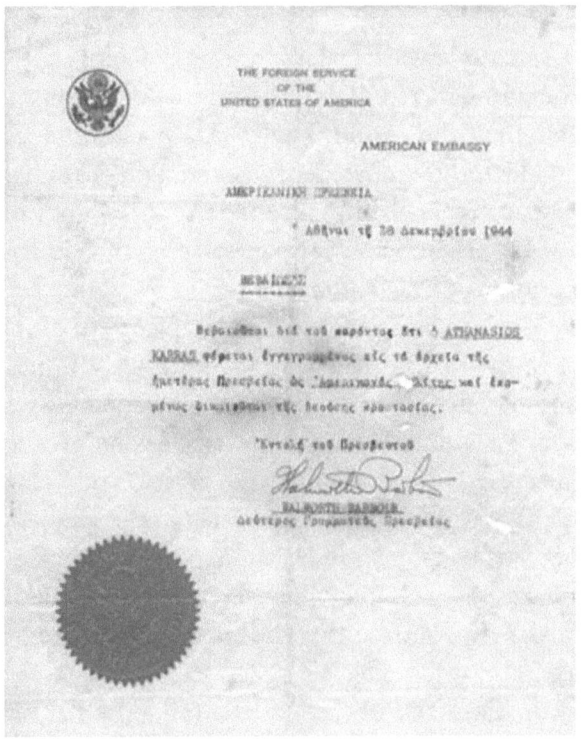

This letter identifies me as an American citizen. It was
issued by the American Consulate in Athens on the
instructions of the American Ambassador, and states that I
was entitled to all due protections. It was written in Greek
and dated 28 December 1944.

Throughout the occupation, the underground resistance was
persistent and ever-present. No doubt, in my own understanding,
and I would say in the understanding of any objective thinker, the
major initiative and most organization resided in the movement
of the political left. Patriotic sentiment was rampant in all Greek
citizens. It appears that it was expressed sooner and with more
emphasis and articulation by the left. Perhaps this was because of
their pre-existing desire to be at the helm, whether during occupation
or otherwise. The positive feeling of the populace toward most of
the resistance activities was logical. For example, the indignity
that we as Americans endured in the belief that the Germans had
stripped us of our identity, was counteracted by the satisfaction

that there existed a defiant force to negate Nazi arrogance. On the other hand, there was opposition to the ideological position of the left. Therefore, mixed emotions had existed among the Greek people throughout the period. The counterpart to the left-leaning underground liberation movement was the right-leaning liberation movement. Even the enemy occupation forces got involved in the situation, for the obvious reason to serve their own interests. Strong accusations surfaced that the right collaborated with Nazis whose philosophy was opposed to Communism. All of this formed the perfect nexus for the blending together of bitterness, hatred, civil war, and bloodshed. The British became entangled even more after the Germans left. Mazower's book does an excellent job of bringing all these issues to light. And, it is for this reason that I recommend his work for anyone interested in the subject. It may be recalled that I did express a reservation about a point in his book. In simple terms, my position with reference to Mazower is that he ends his work by suggesting that the left-leaning underground did not have aspirations to take over Greece after the end of hostilities and the occupation. Yet, in spite of the influence his outstanding work commands to help uphold that view; I find myself compelled to qualify it. He is fair in expressing his conclusion more as an opinion and not as an outright fact. I agree with that. My position in this writing is that I cannot make a categorical statement; other than to say, I end up with only an overriding *quandary* that nullifies any opinion I might have. My thinking, as it will be seen, stems from having lived through those times. Yet, I must add that my experience is but a mere page of a much larger book. It is a valid page, nevertheless. A page that can be extrapolated to bring out not only facts but also deep-rooted feelings that reach the heart and nudge the soul. Given not only the opportunity, but also a solid and reliable organizational structure, the left-leaning sector might well have found itself in power even by default. The famous "percentages" division of the liberated lands between Churchill and Stalin was of no help to the left side. Britain was to keep the major portion of influence over Greece, compared to that of Russia—a despicable practice of and intrusion in the life of other nations. The reality is that Russia, because of that arrangement, would not have helped the leftist element, and England would have fought against it. This was a clear formula for failure of the left, and under such circumstances the left-leaning liberation movement opted to accept the loss and just hope for the future. Nevertheless, this concession did not happen in a smooth and peaceful way. Some order came later, after a great deal of bloodshed and destruction during the famous "Dekemvriana" (or Bloody December of 1944 that ended on 12 February 1945); and later still, after a second lengthier civil war from 30 March 1946 until 16 October 1949. I shall only describe that December period, because I went through it. I was still in Greece only until September 1945.

Patriotic feeling and repugnance and hatred toward the invaders was a standard condition in every true citizen. There was no disagreement or friction in that area. The dilemma surfaced when deciding where or with whom one would associate in order to serve in the resistance or even to survive in an equitable way. The previous discussion highlights that dilemma: Should one join the left-leaning group that in truth is fighting against the aggressor, but embraces the leftist agenda? Or, should one side with the right; yet, whose reputation was tainted with collaborationist tendencies with Germans who were against the left. Or still more, should one stay unclassified, yet still patriotic but alone for whatever opportunity or adversity that might show up even to survive? One way or another, everyone was trapped into this, during and after the occupation. It was terrible all the time.

On my part, I was in some type of neighborhood activity through friends and schoolmates. It was not quite clear where the origin of the group was. Neither did the group mature to a point where a specific action was to be taken. It was sort of a silent reserve to be called upon when needed. My share of hardware was an Italian helmet from some captured prisoner in the Albanian campaign and a pistol. These came into my possession through the others, passed down from hand to hand. I had concealed the pistol well; but the helmet was in the upstairs walk-in closet between two bedrooms. I mentioned earlier that our family occupied the second and third floors. I need to give a few details about the access to and the interior of the house, because of an incident I will describe later. To reach the second-floor main entrance, we would go up an outside stone-built marble-step stairway (marble is still used in Athens with great frequency) to a veranda enclosed by square glass-panes of typical English style. From the veranda, one would walk up a couple of steps into the dining-room and the-living-room. Past the dining-room was the kitchen and a stairway to the third-floor. And on that floor, were two bedrooms and a walk-in closet between them, and a separate bathroom. That's it. The master-bedroom window faced north, and the other bedroom faced south toward the front gate. Also, on the third floor was a door that exited to a terrace. That space of the terrace was in fact the roof of the second-floor. We often sat out there and also slept under the stars during the pleasant months, if there was no German anti-aircraft shooting going on. Next to our property was a nice home occupied by some high-ranking Fascist officer, his wife and their two young daughters, who were quite reclusive—for good reason, of course, considering how the Greek people felt about them living so well. There were several windows all around the rooms of our home with beautiful far-reaching views in almost every direction, as there were few buildings nearby. I will confess, pedestrian as it sounds, even the bathroom window boasted of a panoramic view (a rarity, I would imagine).

Life at home made things a bit more tolerable. At least we could experience a sense of freedom and decency uncommon in those days when one would go out and about. It was an experience for me similar to relief I would feel visiting the ancient ruins and having the chance to escape the boredom and harsh reality that existed. It was nice for a while. The thirst for news from the outside was a constant. As I stated earlier, ordinary radio was useless as a tool to receive free information. My classmate and friend had an uncle who was a maritime engineer and had taught my friend how to put together a crystal radio. One day after school, my friend invited me to his home and showed me how to do it. Next, I visited Athinas Street at the center of town. This was a veritable flea market. Even today, there is trade of frantic proportions going on there. I was able to buy two old earphones, some copper wire, a few meters of antenna wire, four insulators, and a crystal. I went home and got to work. Privacy is always encouraging to do things that one loves most to do. Well, I shared the bedroom with my brother. He was in agreement. The room became a radio-room. The antenna wire was run in diagonal form across the four ceiling corners where the insulators were anchored. A wire dropped to a desk that I had made for my studies. The copper wire was wrapped around an insulated cylinder, and the extension of that wire was connected to a search needle that was moved around until it hit certain spot on the crystal. When the right contact was reached, it meant the right frequency was achieved. To my surprise, I began to receive Egypt and the Allied armed forces news broadcasts. When music came on, it was the first time that I heard Bing Crosby sing the very popular and perky tune, *Swinging on a Star*, that had lyrics such as, "The pig is an animal with dirt on its face ..." When the main news hour came on, that little contraption became my father's exclusive domain. Every day, there was no way that I could dislodge him from that desk or separate him from those earphones! There was no comparison between the French newspapers and the current up-to-the-hour news coming out of that radio about the world, the European, Russian, and North African, and Pacific campaigns. Victory in North Africa was tantamount to the liberation of Greece. We could taste a bit of freedom again—unrealistic as it was. Times became more normal in a way. We could now at least know what is going on in the world. I have no idea whether anyone outside my room could detect my radio reception. We all just felt warm and cozy in our new-found escape in our own privacy. Wrong! This is not how all that good stuff would stay. Remember what I said earlier: anything could happen at any moment. Well, something did happen. And although everything was stacked up against us in a most serious way, by some unknown power, we were saved from it. But, hey, don't let me kid you: My whole life I've known what that power is! It happened that I was downstairs in the dining-room. My mother was in the kitchen. I do not remember whether my brother and sister were even home. My father was upstairs in the master bedroom lying down in bed in his shorts with one knee up and the other leg crossing over it. His head was on the far end of the bed and he faced the bedroom door. He was reading a magazine, and all around him on the bed were several other similar magazines. All of them were the American *Legion* magazines; and they could be seen even from a distance what they were, as well as the one wide open in front of him. I saw all of this.

Now, the bell rings, at top of the steps outside the veranda glass-pane door. I moved to see who it was and started going down the steps from the dining-room to the veranda. I look through the glass panes, and Alas! Who is standing right outside almost as big as the door? It's a high-ranking Nazi officer with his aide right next to him. His uniform was ornate and he sported the usual crop, which he moved around the way they were trained for an imposing or theatrical effect. I was stunned. Who wouldn't be under those conditions?

Anyway, I arrive at the door and open it. He swaggered in with his sidekick behind him and started barking his German at me. Shocked as I was, I managed a body language conveying that I did not understand. Then, he began to speak in a terrible French (anyone would have concluded the same, hearing him try to speak French with his German accent). My response was the same. His aide remained silent throughout that visit. We had come to an impasse. Then, by some force beyond my reason, I opened my mouth and asked if he spoke English. I will never forget to this day the ice-cold look he cast upon me. It was the meanest countenance that came out of controlled anger. I even sensed the reaction of surprise in his aide. The next moment he consented and at once said that he will inspect the house, and right away he set forth with his aide close behind him. I followed third in line. He went up the steps to the dining-room, he looked around and went to the formal guest-room on the right with a brief look around. He then turned and went to the kitchen. Remember, no one at home knew these two were in the house. Therefore, I will leave it to the reader to decide what the expression of my mother was when she turned around and saw this monster appear before her with the other one behind him. That is another look that I will never forget. He continued without delay to the stairway and up to the third floor. Read all this with care: He gives a brief once-over to the bathroom on the right. Then, he enters the first bedroom. He looks at everything in great detail and runs his eyes over the antenna wires and down to the radio contraption, and his eyes scan the rest of the room. He says nothing. I am following them everywhere. He goes out to the hallway and enters the walk-in closet. He opens all the upright tall doors and looks at all the shelves inside. He looks inside the last door and turns his eyes downward and sees the Italian helmet. He says nothing and leaves that room. He pauses a moment, as he sees the door to the terrace, he opens it and looks out for some time (I'm convinced that something military was going on in his thinking). From there he proceeds into the master bedroom, shocks the life out of my father, and observes in detail the American Legion magazines sprawled all over the bed. He scans the whole room and says nothing. He leaves there and goes downstairs. Just before exiting the veranda door ready to depart, he turns around to me and says: "You are going to be out of this house in two hours." That was it.

My mother had gone upstairs to my father, both not knowing about his ultimatum. I ran upstairs at once. I told my parents what he had said. Within moments my father got dressed and bolted out of the house. What happened is that he went straight to the owner. The first floor below was left empty after the French diplomat's departure. The owner did not want to have any occupation military in that house at all. Whatever the procedure was, my father returned home within the two-hour period with a six-by-eight card in hand from the Foreign Affairs Department of the Swiss Consulate in Athens stating that two American citizens under its protection resided there (it only named my brother and me, I believe for brevity and effect). The card was posted outside on the front heavy metal gate, which we had also locked. Within a short period, a couple was brought in and occupied the first floor. It turns out that the couple were diplomats of the Swiss Consulate itself in Athens. And I believe the gentleman was the same white-haired Swiss Consul who stood by on the side of the table when our documents were confiscated by the Nazis at the basement-theater. The couple kept very much to themselves. It makes sense since their role was neutrality.

When the two hours were up, that German did indeed return in his jeep-like vehicle with his driver. A military truck followed him carrying other personnel and bedding equipment. He did not know what was awaiting him until he walked up the ramp of the driveway to the locked gate. We had closed tight all the wooden shutters, and through the cracks of the lowered louvers, up on the third floor, we could see the gate at the front end of the garden. After reading the card we had posted, he started pacing to-and-fro in great anger, snapping his crop on his boot time and time again with fury. At the end of his ordeal, he got back into his vehicle and left. The big point is that we never heard from him or from anyone else again. The protection we had received was most powerful because that character could have destroyed us, having seen all those incredible things in our home. Remember, my brother's friend was hung by his thumbs for far less. In closing, I still have the Swiss Consulate card.

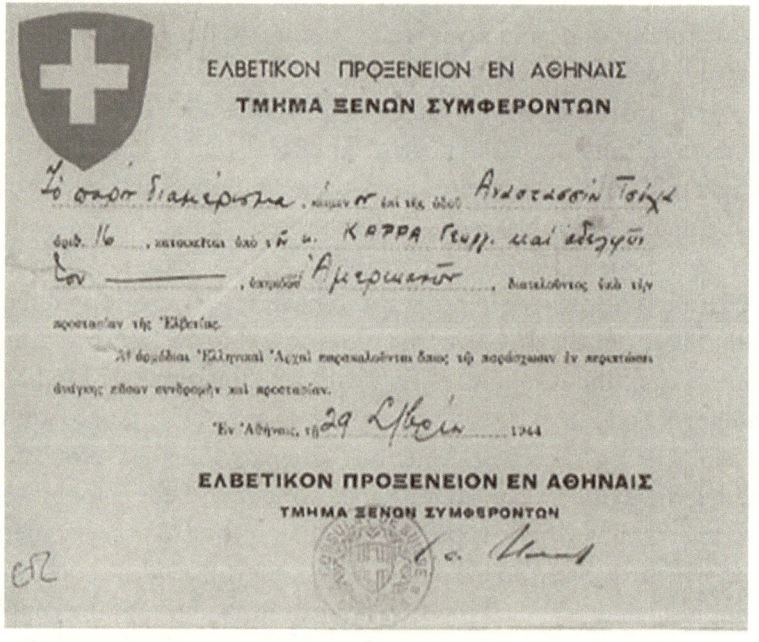

Card displayed at our front gate, was issued by the Swiss Consulate in Athens, that prevented the German from expelling us from our home and moving in himself.

The food shortage and frequent near-starvation saga continued and with time it worsened for everyone. The Germans would steal the food and the people would starve. And, the worse things got for

Hitler in his failing campaigns, the worse it became for the people in Greece. This had brought my father to an impasse. He had to consider that bold steps were needed. My mother's oldest brother (the one who saw me on that German vehicle) had found work at a food distribution center. I don't know details about it, but as I recall he would remark in a negative way concerning the operation and the Germans having a hand in it. I think that there was also black-market hanky-panky going on. It is not surprising, considering all the misery, instability, confusion, hatred, misinformation, suffering, and death that filled both the space and the atmosphere. It was the normal of the times. This is why I say that wheeling and dealing is what people had to do. Of course, even in normal times, effort is needed in order to survive. Life is not for free. But, the lowered quality of social standards, the uncertainty, and the intensity of effort were far more taxing in those times. Through my uncle's job, his wife also began to work for some type of philanthropic food activity. These occupations gave to both of them small allowances of food that they could bring home to their family. This was an occasional source of food that they shared with us. I mention all this as an example of the kind of improvisation people had to engage in.

As a tangible solution, my father had decided to leave the family in Athens and by himself go to our summer home in the mountains and try to gather any food items and supplies that he could to bring back. He refused to be accompanied by my brother or me. This was a very bold decision fraught with risks. Chief among the dangers were those nasty road blocks he would have to face: Who was he? Where did he come from? Where was he going? Why was he going? And if the answers didn't match, what then? My opinion is that he would have ended up either on a truck or on a train en route to Germany as forced labor or as a victim of the macabre good Doctor Josef Mangele as a human experiment—and I know about both of these. Yes, I do. I was later stationed in Germany during the Cold War and assigned to the US Constabulary Brigade; a military body organized to help implement the investment of the Marshall Plan for Europe's reconstruction. In essence, it was a military police unit dedicated to the reestablishment of civil, organizational, and administrative order in post-war dismantled Germany. The unit functioned for six years from 1946 to 1952 and then deactivated. More road mileage was recorded for jeep usage by the Constabulary during that period than for the entire war just ended. My assignment was in Munich. Dachau is nearby. There I met with Greek men and women who had served time as laborers for the Nazis and had remained, finding new opportunities with the arrival of the Allies. Also, here are my first cousin's words to me concerning her uncle, whom I knew as well from before the war. She writes, "1945!!! You were in Japan. I was 3 years old ... My uncle Yannis (my mother's brother) was in Dachau. Was saved by the Americans after he escaped from the camp hospital, sick and in a very bad condition because they had removed his kidney for medical experiments. What times ..." (She mentions Japan, knowing I served there in the US Army 25th Division. I was drafted and served in Japan after my arrival from Greece and right after the few months of high school in Miami. Later, I served again in the Korean War, but I was assigned in Germany). My cousin's remarks above are not a mere nebulous anecdote, but a solid account of what happened. As stated, her uncle was captured by the Nazis and sent to Dachau as slave labor to work at the BMW motor-building plant. He was later used under normal health conditions as a human guinea pig for medical experiments by having his left kidney removed. A report in his own handwriting describing his ordeal and escape from the camp hospital appears on a wall in Dachau. He relates his subsequent liberation by the Americans who helped him recover from near-death because of exhaustion and infection, which later they controlled with penicillin. Yannis Stathopoulos was a Greek Patriot and Freedom Fighter.

The bottom line is that my father did make it through, both ways. Although, the physical demand on him had its toll—not right then: Later, but very early in his life, when he was back home in the States, we lost him. It is more than justifiable for me to consider him my hero; and not just alone that he is my father. He somehow found the way to reach our mountain place. There, for a three-month period he toiled, not used to the hardship of rural life and unaccustomed to hand labor. He managed to gather a variety of foodstuff—wheat, corn, raisins, walnuts, and whatever else he garnered and brought it all home. I am sure he must have obtained some items from the locals as well. Then, he put the stuff in burlap bags and started on his way back. For me, this was an incredible achievement. How did he make it through those road blocks? Those Germans and Italians had no pity for any Greek. And in particular, Germans who were hard-bent on stripping Greece of its food supply. I cannot imagine that they would let through a quantity of food such as the one my father had collected. Yet, he did it. For certain, what came through was his Greek ingenuity and his American business know-how. He put them both to use and he made it. One day, two Italian military trucks showed up at that unforgettable front gate. Four or so boisterous, half-drunk, good-time Italians dismounted and next to them my father. What a sight! They helped him unload his burlap bags, and then continued bringing down some small wooden crates. By that time, my brother and I joined the effort. The trucks stayed in the street, and we carried things to the house on foot, and then up the steps to the dining-room where there was ample space. What was the extra load, besides the bags that we brought up? To our surprise, we carted in three hundred empty Chianti-wine bottles—the round-bottom type with the basket weave, that can be stood up! Yes, all empty—three hundred of them! There you have it.

My father had struck a deal with these happy-go-lucky... soldiers: To bring him to his home safe and sound with all his goods, and in exchange he would buy from them all those empty bottles. Such a deal!... as my Jewish friends would say. They got their money (inflationary as it was) and went off their merry way; and we got our food supply along with three hundred empty Chianti-wine bottles (that somehow, we got rid of later, because they didn't stay in our home too long. And, what a pity on that score: Today they would have been collectibles, and they could have brought twenty dollars per bottle, they say!). The mystery here is, how did those Italians manage to get through the check points on the arterial road they traveled to enter Athens? Did my father keep buying bottles from all of them? And, what about the Germans? It isn't as though Greece had long-distance alternative routes. As far as I know, even now it is difficult in such a mountainous country. Try it. Kudos to my father! (And to think: some want to get rid of the free-enterprise system).

All good and well for what happened above. Yet, meat, chocolate, coffee, sugar, fresh vegetables, fruits, cheese, yogurt, and above all olive oil, and other nutritional items, also medications, all remained in the dream stage or in one's imagination rather than a tangible reality. Nevertheless, we were thankful for what we had. Often one will observe people who will not leave the table with food still in their plate, which can be thrown away. My guess is that such persons have gone through a war or have experienced hunger in other circumstances. I still continue to clean my plate, even if it is considered...poor etiquette. It is arrogance of the first order to regard one's self above the possibility of someday finding one's self in that very predicament. And besides, it reflects utter inhumanity not to consider that at the very moment many others are experiencing abject hunger for one reason or another. To begin with, food does not fall from the sky. It may have happened once in human history, but it was for other specific reasons. Food production is not easy. It does not command value only because it feeds and nourishes, but also because it requires creative labor and effort to produce it. Food should not be wasted any more than water should. It should not be taken for granted, and it is not guaranteed to anyone, including the wealthy. The principle applies to other items; yet, for the moment the reference is to food. Need of any sort is a lesson in wisdom. The new generations should always defer to previous human experience. Often, this can prevent repetition of errors that cause re-living hardships that teach the same lessons. Regression is wasteful and foolish. And, as it was stated earlier, the practice of preserving previous experiences and applying the choice ones, is the sure road to better culture and civilization. To be modern does not mean to demolish everything that is received from the past. It means, to use everything that is best from the past, and from that to produce something that will be good for the future. Anyone coming out of the ravages of that war (or similar circumstances) is more conscious of the principles mentioned here.

The hazards in Greece continued. To be in the streets (let alone what could happen at home as we saw) was always risky. The villages and countryside suffered horrific conditions as well, not only Athens or the other large towns. Mass executions of civilians and burning of settlements took place all over. The usual and handy excuse by the Nazis was that these were reprisals or that people were shot for running away. The word was all over about a German who wanted to show a subordinate how to shoot Greeks who ran away. He demonstrated by going behind a random individual, kicked the person hard in the rear, caused the person to pace forward and then shot him in the back. He then explained that this was how it's done. The longer occupation went on, the worse it got. Hitler had his hands full with repeated military losses, and the more this happened the more insane he became. This reflected down the line as officers and men became more callous and immune to conscience. The uglier and the crueler the better they thought, in combating the underground resistance. The whole matter fed upon itself, as the resistance continued. Besides all the killings, Germans also engaged in rounding up civilians. The purpose was to herd them off to Germany or to other locations to be used as slave labor or for medical experiments as we have seen. The practice of rounding up people was a terrifying experience. It would happen at an unexpected time and at any place in the streets without any prior indication. Their method was very effective how they did it and for the terror it was designed to produce. The Greeks called the activity, the "bloko" and in the plural the "bloka." This was the Greek phonetic rendition of the word, "block." Here is what happened to me, and this will describe how the method worked in Athens, or elsewhere for that matter: Things were running along in a quiet way, except for the occasional outburst of personal spats and the like. At the flea market area, the noise and the foot traffic were more pronounced as usual. The stores in general were a poor version of their former vibrancy before the war. The only traffic I can remember as the busiest was the electric streetcars on the rails. Otherwise, there was the German and Italian military traffic; the loudest and most irritating of which was the occasional little German vehicle fueled with burning wood— making an intolerable racket. There was no shortage of pedestrians as always in Athens. People would come and go for whatever their reasons. A city is a city even during the occupation. One can see similar activity in other cities of Europe, as in films about Paris, for example. People are milling about in normal ways. There may be need for food, for clothing, for entertainment or whatever; but, in simple terms, life continued. This, is why the experience being described is so shocking. The sudden change of events is overpowering and paralyzing. There is no time given to react. As a matter of fact, any sudden move can spell doom; unless one is prepared to gamble it all. To put it in very common words: In a situation of a bloko it is best not to be a smart-aleck. The unfortunate thing is that one loses either way. I explain: People are active in the street. Military vehicles, small and big, are present any time. They all look the same. It happens that one of them of the bigger size, while going at a normal city speed and appearing to move along, stops cold. In a split second, several Germans jump out of the back and start fanning out in all directions. They have rifles and automatic guns aimed at the public while running. They stop and turn around facing the center, where some of their own are posted looking all around. The ones outside stretch their arms and begin to close the circle. Some may reach and join hands. Anyone caught inside the circle is finished— he or she is now theirs. And I mean theirs. People disappeared that way and were never seen or heard from again. There is your bloko. And, if you think of being a smart-aleck and run, you are sure to get it in the back—remember, the Germans loved justifying themselves that way in the eyes of international law: They shot you in the back because you ran. I was in Omonia that day for some reason. Don't ask me why. The most plausible reason is that I had been at Athinas at the flea market that was nearby. I remember the exact spot where I stood. It was near the center where a pre-war fanning fountain with colored lighting used to be, and on the side across from a restaurant where Tritis Septemvriou Boulevard begins. I was facing toward the restaurant (our family used to dine there), when the incident took place. It happened in the wide area between the restaurant, the street, and the spot across the street where I was. As I stood there, two German hands touched right in front of me! Had they been behind me ... What then? There could be variations of this in terms of who they targeted, the reason they did it, the number they wanted captured, the fate of those they captured (kill, imprison, send off as slave labor), and all such. I can only testify to that which I experienced myself that day. Captives were also subject to being shot on the spot.

Then again, how could life go on if people were unable to leave their homes? One way or another, people have to exit their homes and be in the streets for multiple reasons. Even if we discount the normal possibility of mishaps, accidents, crimes, and the like when folks are away from home; it was still not possible to predict when the occupiers would act. The only thing certain was that both Germans and Italians increased the possibility of someone being hurt when out in the streets. Let's remember what I experienced the night with the French newspapers and the Italians and with the bloko I just related—both sudden, unexpected, and unpredicted incidents. I was not the only one by any means. Yet, it is my own experiences I am describing in this account. The occupiers were not kind enough to publish their attack schedule in advance, so folks could adjust their own timing to avoid the hazards. That was the whole idea behind the unpredictability: which is the constant anticipation of danger by the public in order to keep everyone off guard and submissive. This method diminished the need for their troops to be on guard everywhere and at all times. The public fear of where and when the sword would drop did the job for them. Their human and operational cost decreased and they kept doing it more and more. The sad reality is that they succeeded to a measurable degree. What happened over time is that the people started to become fatalistic—so to speak, if it comes it comes. What can one do about it? In addition—and this is even sadder—not only the occupiers, but also the people to some degree started to become callous and tolerant of criminality; which means, that the threshold of humanity and civility was being lowered to the level of the Fascists and Nazis. This should be a compelling lesson for humanity today: To obliterate terrorism in its root; because, if it is allowed to continue, it will soon become the standard and accepted way of life. Mass killings of human beings will be considered as expected events, because of the converted perception that life is normal that way. Whether my own standards had dropped is hard for me to tell. When one is in deep waters, one does not know the depth. Reliable information must come from an independent source. I do know that I was in the midst of it all and that I was adjusting to it. This makes me believe that my very adjustment formed the lowering of my own threshold. Why not? I was no different than anyone else. And, nor was anyone else. I had to be outside, whether a lot or a little. Perhaps I had no business that day to be at the Athinas Street flea market. On the other hand, maybe I had good reason, seeing that I had a crystal radio to maintain. And just because I was there, it was not I who instigated the bloko. After all, it came to me. I wasn't looking for it. The point in all this is that one had to live one's life with the added hazard of the Nazis and Fascists around. And there it is, a touch of fatalism as well. Now, going to school is another story. At least, no one can blame me or any other student for being in the streets in that case. By no means am I echoing any guilt about myself in all I convey above. To the contrary, I am saying that I felt positive about myself in living my life as I pleased, free of some pathetic little personality such as Hitler or Mussolini who thought of themselves superior to others—typical of all similar individuals when given excessive importance. The Greeks had it right with their memorable popular tunes ridiculing Mussolini with their lyrics. They would have labeled the other too (Hitler), had pre-invasion time been longer.

Whenever school was available there was often talk about this thing happening and another thing happening, and so on and so forth. Maybe the grapevine exaggerated much. The fact is, where there is smoke there is fire; since in most instances events had happened. The situation was constant upheaval and often reason to dismiss class and go home to avoid some danger. In addition, as I had mentioned earlier, the presence of not only the students, but also of the professors was not always certain. The reason is clear: Teachers too were part of the public with families, homes, obligations, needs such as food, and subject to risking the streets as anyone else. Often enough there was disorganization because of their economic situation. Pay systems in a mess, and adding inflation to that, caused teachers to pursue other forms of survival activity away from their profession. And, not to exclude the patriotic and the political issue in which they too would get involved. All of this combined shows how the educational system had been affected.

At this point I will stand in solid defense of Greece's educational accomplishment during that terrible period. Suffice it to say that my total high-school education was only three and a half years (out of six years in the Greek system—compared to three and three in the US). The reason, of course, was the interruptions. My brother had done a little better, as he was one year older and had already one more year under his belt. My sister too was subjected to the same problem. The three and a half years I earned in Greece were enhanced by another half year of high school in Miami on my return home—although a bit older than normal. I must add that even those three and a half years credited to me in Greece had not been continuous. The education we received, in spite of the interruptions and brevity, earned for my brother admission to MIT with honor-student status in one of those years. And for me, it earned admission to Columbia University in New York. On completion of my sophomore year at Columbia, the undergraduate School of Business was discontinued. Only the graduate level became available. Some of those undergraduates were granted direct admission to the graduate level. I was one of them.

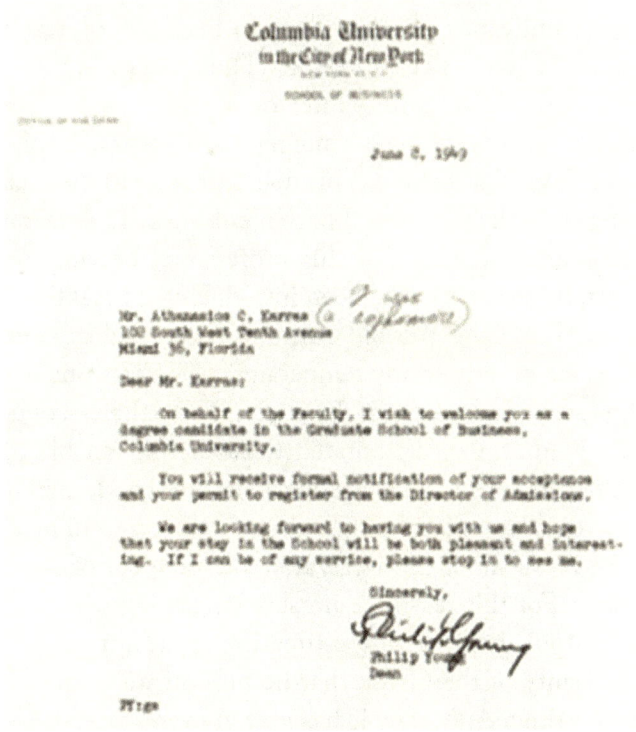

Acceptance letter to the Graduate School of Business, Columbia University in 1949, while only a sophomore.

Circumstances did not permit me to continue and I withdrew (most unfortunate). Nonetheless, I earned my MA in Economics much later from the University of Miami, after my return from Chile where I had resided for several years. My mention of all this is as a testimonial to the educational quality in Greece in those years, notwithstanding the dislodging actions of Hitler and Mussolini.

The following account will give a more vivid picture of how schooling was affected in those times. It will be made clearer how random interruptions and events happened that disturbed the educational system in so many major ways. Day by day, as stated, school attendance by both students and teachers worsened. The classroom would look different each day, depending on who showed up among the students and the teachers. Class composure began to be loose. Sessions were cancelled or rescheduled. And this was high school where more discipline is required, as compared to university flexibility—more so in the Greek system that was very strict. Such conditions were unheard of before. Even in high school, teachers carried an aura of university professors. Their public status was high and they enjoyed community esteem.

One teacher, who was much younger than others, displayed signs of escape from that format. This does not refer to the quality of his teaching or to the strictness I have mentioned. The reference is to his dress appearance and to his professorial bearing, so to speak. In short, he seems to have been introducing a breakthrough of modernism, displacing the old cultural habits and etiquettes. That had its value and fitted my temperament. He was one of the teachers who referred to me as an American. Nevertheless, outside of his impact in that area, I hesitated to favor him on his open effort to modify the Greek language. He advocated modernizing it, if you will, by removing many of the rules of grammar and making the written form too simple. He was, after all, professor of classical Greek language. For this reason, I am sure that along with others, his innovation took hold. In my estimation, gone forever is the richness and beauty of the Greek that he himself was required to teach me at the time. And, now it has gotten even worse, because of the compromises made in order to accommodate the electronic digital versions. That was the down side. Next, I will describe why, when I returned to Greece for the first time after thirty-nine years, I sought him out and went to express my gratitude to him. And, I will explain why the Greek language alone was not the reason for my appreciation.

As time went by, more and more he was the one teacher that would always show up. I believe it was only one time that he missed coming in, and it was because he had taken ill. I remember it, on account of the confusion and anxiety that ran through the school that day. Fear and doubt were always present. That day the question right away became, what happened to him? Did he have a clash with the Germans or the Italians? Was it a problem his family might have had with them? Did he get hurt in the streets? The odd thing is that, nobody considered the simple possibility he may not be feeling well. And of course, that's what it was. In those days, the most feared was suspected. And that was what the Germans wanted. Anyway, the teacher did show up a day or two later. School continued, and one day an ultimatum came down shocking the entire school.

The building was a former two-story spacious home that the school system had gotten and with few changes made it a very fitting school. The many rooms were now classrooms. Outside in the back was an adequate patio nestled among the other buildings. That was where we took our session breaks. We could not go out front because it would be a downtown street. The wooden benches were for each student a stool and a desk as a set. They were comfortable because the stools could be shifted. The ultimatum was curt and dry, issued by the Italian military, that we be out by the next day. In effect, they were taking over our school and making it their barracks. And Kolonaki, where our school was, is still the elegant section of Athens. The Italian army there? Yes, that's what they were doing. Does this seem similar to the German ordering us out of our home?

There was pandemonium. The stairway got crowded with students running upstairs and down, trying to find out from someone what to do. The questions were: What do we do now? Where do we go? When will school start again? Who is going to let us know? Then, the young professor took the lead. His voice rang out from the top of the stairs, loud and clear. He said for everyone at once to grab their stool and their desk and anything they can carry. Take them home with them and leave right away. Stay in touch with each other every day and wait until we would hear from him. He added, each of us to speak with our parents to gather funds for renting a space. That was it. In just a few minutes that building was bare. Well done. We found out later he was informed the Italians planned to use the desks for fire to keep warm.

As I said, things were getting nastier and nastier by the day. We all followed his instruction, and one day I got the word that school was going to be near the area of Pangkrati. This was farther away for me than the previous location. I didn't mind the walking anyway. What he ended up doing was to rent a vacant one-room mom-and-pop corner store. This was about a twenty-by-twenty-foot single room with just the front door that cut across the corner in a diagonal facing the sidewalk corner. It made for a pretty wide entrance that used a metal roll-up door. When the shutter was rolled up, there was a regular door with wide glass panes to see in or out. In other words, it was a regular store-front. When the metal panel was rolled down, one could not see in or out. I describe this for a reason. It took about two weeks to hear from the teacher. The good thing was that on my way to the new school, I went right by my friend's home—the one with the crystal radio. From his home, we would go back and forth together the rest of the way.

The classroom we put together at that little store was to be remembered. As one can imagine, the room looked spacious when it was empty. But, when the desks arrived it became very small. So, we had crowded the desks and the stools so near each other that when looking down, one could not see the floor. We walked on top of the desks to go to our seats in the back of the room. Teaching went on anyway. Even a blackboard had been carried away from the former school. And here is another interesting arrangement. Three teachers participated rotating their schedules, so each can teach their own subject. This method lasted for a while. Soon though, two of those teachers stopped attending. The young one remained steady as ever. And he not only taught us ancient Greek, his subject, but came prepared to teach us math as well. Thirty-nine years later

I made the special effort to meet him again, and I did. I invited him to lunch and he accepted on condition that he would select the location. Of course, I agreed; and I am glad I did, because he chose a restaurant at the foot of the Acropolis with a spectacular view of the Parthenon from below (and an even more dramatic view at night when it is illuminated—I've been there again after that first time). I was informed later that the architect of that location happened to be one of my cousins, growing up together.

The saga about that converted store does not end here. School went on with its ups and downs. One day, while class was on, a lot of shooting started. It did not seem close, but it was quite loud and massive. None of us knew what it was about, including the teacher. Our class was interrupted as we sat there trying to figure out what to do. Soon enough, some people hurried by on the sidewalk in front of the store or class. They came from the direction my friend and I would take to go home. As they went by they said that the Germans had hanged several people. And they added that the underground guerillas had come down the hills to recover the bodies and the Germans resisted. The shooting continued and seemed to come closer. So, at once we rolled down the metal shutter and only left a sliver of an opening at the bottom to see out. The place looked closed up. A short time later, we heard running approach and the sound of metal-cleat shoes go by. We could see the feet of those who ran by on the sidewalk in front of the store, but not who they were. It may have been guerillas or Greek security whom the Germans controlled. Either way, we stayed quiet for about an hour. Outside, there was total silence. We began discussing what to do. It was certain we could not stay there. We all decided to go home. It was the usual pattern anyway. First a lot of commotion with damage and lots of hiding, then complete silence, and then dispersing and going home. Almost routine. My friend and I knew our destination and without words started our way home. In front of us the unknown. Yet, everything was normal and peaceful. His home came up first. He lived on a rather busy street, on the left side as we approached. Past his front door another four doors was a cross street. At that corner, his own road was split. Part of it continued straight and part of it veered off to the right.

This split at that location made for a sharp corner in the building and the sidewalk. The whole arrangement, therefore, was right outside his home. Now, he and I were coming up his street at yet some distance from his front door. Sometimes we separated there, and other times we went to the next street behind his home. He did that for quick access through his neighbor's yard to a room in his own back yard. It was where he did all his studying and hobbies. Either way, I would bid him *yassou* and continue on my way. At a given moment, we spotted some minor activity at that sharp corner. We decided to go the back way. So as usual, we turned left at the next cross street and then right again. When we reached his neighbor's home, he asked if I wanted to stay (sometimes I did for a few moments). I refused, thinking my family would be worried. He went off through the yard, and I continued on. Then, when I reached the corner of the cross street, it happened: A German, hiding around the corner, jumped out in front of me, his hefty automatic pointed and pressed against my gut, agitated, a little taller than I, blue eyes, his face about a foot away from mine, looked me in the eye, as well I did him, held there silent for maybe three-four seconds. In those brief moments, he was master of all options: He could have hit me. He could have barked at me. He could have even smiled at me. And worst of all, he could have shot me, and his whole problem would have been solved. All it would have been is just another case in the streets. No one would have questioned him. The field was his to control. The result was, he chose to bark. He pulled back his gun and shouted, *Raus!* (Scram!). That was my cue. For a split moment, as my eyes were released from his, I happened to be looking in the direction of the sharp corner. I caught a glimpse of two bodies hanging from the sidewalk trees. Next, in a stupor (the best I can describe), I started walking with a controlled pace (as if to be on best behavior). And when I rounded the corner, I started running. To begin with, he was agitated. He had a weapon, I didn't. He could have changed his mind at any moment. Remember? Shot in the back because he ran. Nothing had value. The whole environment felt filthy. I always thought he let me go only because he looked me in the eye face-to-face. Nothing else makes sense. He could not have processed facts in his mind in that short a time—whether I was a resistance member or not, what I looked like, or just because I came up the street in a casual manner. He could not have trusted any of that. His own life was at stake. He had just finished defending himself against the guerillas. He would always choose on the side of his own safety. Anyway, that was the spot where all the shooting happened, and the German was one of the guards. It was not only two people hanged. It was five. I visited that corner many years later. The municipality has placed a plaque on the wall of that sharp corner, listing the names of all five persons. It's still there.

Plaque on Xenias Street in Athens memorializing the five persons hanged there by the Germans with their collaborators on 5 April 1944.

It was hard at times to believe that major hazards or final moments were not close by. Anybody in similar circumstances or in a combat zone will tell you the same. It's so in normal life as well. The main difference is the intensity and frequency with which hazards are happening. For example, I recall walking in open space on unpaved ground and I heard a blunt sound on the ground right next to me. What do you think it was? It was a piece of shrapnel dropping from the sky. I bent down and picked it up. It was a jagged nasty-looking piece of metal about two inches long and half inch wide. I still have it. Anti-aircraft firing was frequent. This must have come from one of the exploded shells. Allied aircraft would fly by (no doubt from North Africa) going north, and the Germans shot at them. People knew that bombs would not fall from Allied aircraft, so they were outside. But, shrapnel did fall. It was wiser not to be outside. It had become routine and people defied much. Callousness and fatalism...Remember? By the way, people became aeronautical engineers too. We knew that Allied aircraft had a winding drone. The German kind was continuous. When the Allied ones went by, we were all awake and outside at night watching the fireworks. Bad advice.

The bottom line in all of this? There are no heroes, just people scrambling around to survive. Some survive and some perish. That's the symptom. And who is the cause of it all? The people themselves. Yet, we must dig deeper. At the start of this writing these words appear: "So, let's probe ahead and visit events, which in turn caused other events..." The question, therefore, must be asked: What is there that causes people to do what they do to themselves? I don't profess to be one to give the answer to this difficult question. I do feel it is reasonable to say that not only one, but multiple causes underlie the nature of human behavior. On a case by case search we can identify some of them. One can be recognized as the ideological factor. That is, how people believe human society must govern itself so everyone has a fair existence. This means that people either want to live as free creative individuals, or as cooperative members of a society. Or, they want to reject all individual obligations and responsibilities and let a central authority take over and rule the society. In simpler terms, this means two systems: a free capitalist system and a socialist system. The first allows individual freedom and initiative with cooperation for the total good of the society. The second deprives individual freedom and initiative but obligates the central authority to care for all the society. Both systems are imperfect and both must be maintained by society. The first runs the risk of all wealth and power being concentrated in the hands of few who may control the society. The second runs the risk of the central authority likewise controlling all wealth and power and that society. The critical issue here is that: One system allows free individual action and initiative; the second deprives individual freedom of action for the sake of relief from responsibility. People are at odds over this difference and how they want to live. This is one cause that sets people apart and that leads them to the type of behavior I have so far described. Nazis had their own way of life, Bolsheviks had theirs, Capitalists had theirs, and so on. Greeks as well had their own convictions and found themselves divided in a deep struggle that bred animosity and hatred. The condition was also fueled and aggravated by the Germans, the Russians, and the British—through the actual presence in Greece of the Germans and the British, and through the Communists of Greece as Russian surrogates.

This brings us to the second phase of my experiences, because a civil war erupted in Greece after the retreat of the Germans. In the context of the war and the occupation, the Greek internal struggle had begun early after the surrender of Greece to the Axis. It was carried on within the very resistance movement and became a dilemma throughout the occupation. I will not venture into the complex issues of that period. Mazower's book is the exact source one should use if interested in the subject. My writing here is focused on the description of my personal experiences during that period. I should note that my exposure to that struggle only lasted till September 1945, when I returned home to the States with my brother. Our parents with our sister came back six months later. The struggle in Greece lasted until 16 October1949 when it came to an end with the American intercession of the Truman Doctrine, which started on 12 March 1947 (the Truman Doctrine later evolved into the Marshall Plan for all Europe). My friend and classmate (my radio pal) went through the entire war and occupation unscathed, only to be wounded in that struggle, and yet he survived.

TIME OF LIBERATION

THE CROSSROADS AT THE Kifissias and Alexandras central streets is without doubt an arterial location in Athens. Already described is the surrender of Athens that happened there, as well that Marathon runners transit the place. The Germans had entered there. On liberation, the British too came in the same way, at least from one direction that I can attest to. Kifissias becomes Vassilissis Sofias at the intersection with Alexandras, and continues to Syntagma Square, where the Greek Parliament is located, and where the very well-known and popular Evzons stand guard at the Tomb of the Unknown Soldier. One block south of Alexandras and running parallel to it was the street where our home was located. By exiting our front gate to the left and going about three quarters of a long block, I would meet Vassilissis Sofias, where our street ended. And right there, across Vassilissis Sofias is still the Ippokration Hospital that the Germans occupied. In those days, there were not as many structures as there are now. A person standing at that location and looking north toward Alexandras, would have a very clear view of the main intersection. All those were my stomping grounds. One way or another I would always be there milling around—whether going to the streetcar terminal to go to school, running an errand, visiting friends, or whatever. One day I was taken by a great surprise. It was the sequel, so to speak. of having been present when the Germans entered Athens. In a truest sense, I had witnessed their front end—that is, seeing them come into the city. On the day I am now describing, I watched their rear end in literal physical terms as they were leaving. I had just arrived at Vassilissis Sofias on our street. They had abandoned the hospital and lined up in formation on Vassilissis Sofias to my right. They began to march toward Syntagma Square. The very last equipment in that formation was a water-tank mounted on two wheels and hauled by a vehicle. And the very last Germans were two men following on either side of the water-tank with rifles strapped on their shoulders. I had all the time in the world to watch them march away farther and farther. I kept looking and taking it all in. I watched the one on the left and then the other on the right. And last (this is still so vivid in my memory), my eyes were fixed on the canteen on the one on the right. He carried it on back of his right hip. As he marched, the canteen hit his derrière and was bopping up and down. It made for a comical sight. That was the dignity of the Third Reich for me. The "Raus" imperative had switched and fell on the Nazis themselves. That's the last I ever saw of such Germans. In my mind, that canteen is still bopping and bopping.

Here is more. The jubilation was almost without end that day. While watching the Germans retreat, I heard the increasing roar of a crowd coming from the main intersection. My attention turned in that direction. As I said, I had a clear view of that area from where I was. The crowds were gathering from one moment to the next and the roar was getting louder. I had no idea what was happening. It wasn't as though there was organization and public information service that would broadcast or circulate the latest news to the public. Everything was segmented, confusing, and scrambled with sections of the city differing in their knowledge of what was happening elsewhere It was almost always word of mouth and a lot of rumors. I am certain that few people knew what I saw the Germans were doing. I just happened in that case to have a front-row view. And neither did I know what was going on elsewhere. Moments later, when I went home, it was clear that my family had no idea what was happening. All that commotion at the intersection was because the British were entering the city from the same direction as the Germans had. As I looked, two civilian buses came down Kifissias, and instead of continuing straight at the intersection, they made a right turn on Alexandras and proceeded to the city center that way. Had they gone straight, they would have clashed head-on with the Germans, who as I explained were retreating at a snail's pace. This of course had all been prearranged between the Allies and the Germans. There was an agreement in place that the Germans would not try to defend their position in Athens and that they would withdraw without fighting. They were getting battered enough elsewhere. Their retreat without fighting was not because they were being nice. They had acted as savages all the time there. It was because they were scared of the Russians cutting them off in the Balkans and they were rushing to get out. Further on this matter of the agreement, there were other prevailing issues that existed. An extraordinary arrangement some time in 1944 in Lisbon between Britain and Germany, at a higher than the diplomatic level, provided as follows: Greece would remain under British influence in exchange for the safety of the German troops while in Greece and during their subsequent withdrawal. A German troop transfer in full armament from the islands to the mainland of Greece took place in plain sight of the British navy in the Aegean. Another German contingent in western Crete still remained as an independent zone of influence in case Greece yielded to Communism—and it was contemplated that this western section would be separate and independent of Greece. The act highlights the contradiction of the times and the quandary that I mentioned earlier and to which I will refer again later. It must be noted that a separation of that sort never came to pass, and Crete remained and still forms an integral part of Greece. Typical practice of creating myths to legitimize the taking away of lands, possessions, art, etc. is the claim of a British officer that the people of Crete were of Doric blood and therefore not Greek. He compared them to the rest of the population that he claimed were Greek because they were Pelasgians (Dorians and Pelasgians, of course, were in close proximity in ancient times). Under those conditions, he postulated that since they were not Greek, they should be a separate territory, apart from the rest of the Greeks. In this fashion, he concluded that the German armed military contingent could remain there without occupying any part of Greece! Yet, in terms of an honest appraisal he also failed to submit that both Herodotus and Pausanias were very explicit about the Dorians being Greeks. That people migrated from northern Greece to the south, occupying Peloponnesus, Crete, Rhodes and other islands, the east coast of Asia Minor and also Sicily. Meanwhile, for a full nine-month period past the liberation of Athens (12 October 1944), the British bided time while the German armed unit (17,000 strong) remained in Crete until July 1945. The aim of the said officer was to subject Crete as an independent state to the British orbit—something like Australia, he claimed. No doubt that wartime does dredge up all sorts of elements. Think of it this way: the Greek people had just gotten rid of the Fascists and the Nazis. And by the way, Crete was the last place in the world to see the swastika lowered and trashed on 23 May 1945; while the Germans who had occupied the island were ferried off in British ships—which is to say that heroic (by earned right) Greece was the last country in the world to be free of the Nazis. The only exception was a swastika flying at a military outpost in the uninhabited, frozen, and desolate Arctic, where nobody could or cared to look at it anyway (noted by Greek author, Andreas Nenedakis).

It was pandemonium at the intersection. The buses were full of British soldiers who were hanging out the windows like in a circus, flailing their arms and waving palm branches they must have gotten somewhere up the road from other folks when they were boarding the buses. The excitement was phenomenal—the screaming, the dancing, the embracing, the laughter, and all sorts of behavior. When I understood what was happening, I made a bee-line home. I was a pretty good runner. Even with the occupation, when energy permitted, I would exercise and run at the National Stadium with others. I also ran in the garden at home because it was pretty expansive. There was a rather tall grapevine structure where I did many chin-ups often, and I was pretty good with roller skates, jumping over chairs and the like. I never took to soccer or basketball, although I did play soccer every now and then. When I got home all excited and anxious, I was not believed by my family. They were telling me to be careful what I said and to quiet down. It took a few moments for them to accept what I was saying, when the crowds increased on Alexandras and the noise began to be heard at home. Also, looking out the windows from the third floor, it was clear that there was extraordinary activity in the streets. The news began to fan out to the neighborhoods and soon the whole city was transformed. The elation is difficult to describe. When I went downtown and mingled with the crowds at Syntagna Square in front of the Grande Bretagne Hotel, I felt the atmosphere had changed. The sky was no longer grey. I say this all the time, and I have heard others say it. And it was not because of the clouds. Grey clouds had nothing to do with it. For me, out of all of this, including the joy I shared with so many others on liberation at Syntagma Square, there is something else exclusive and a special privilege. That is: I stood at the spot where I witnessed the Germans take over Athens and thus Greece. And again, I stood at a spot where with my own eyes at one and the same time I witnessed both the Germans retreat from Athens and the Allies enter Athens, symbolic of the liberation of Greece. I saw no other pedestrians in any direction within my line of vision, except for the crowds up at the main intersection. I stood there at that crossroad alone. This can never be matched, and I am thankful for it and consider it a special blessing to have been led there at that moment to witness that singular historic event.

CIVIL STRIFE

WHERE WHITE IS, THERE is also black. Day is always followed by night. And in this case, time of joy, laughter and dance also had its opposite. At once, the retributions began. There were sundry ways how this was carried out. Short time after the Germans left, anarchy began to set in. Good or bad, the occupiers were the authority under which society functioned. Their absence left a vacuum that was not filled right away. There was no Greek authority that everyone obeyed and respected. The opposite was true. The rejection to such an authority had already been in place throughout the occupation. And it was this very division that continued after the Germans left; and which became the devastating civil war. Part of the population was on the left and another was on the right. Both also considered themselves patriotic and liberators against the invader, while at the same time fighting each other. We shall pick up on this subject again later. First, let's make few brief remarks about retributions and the lull that was created when the Germans left.

Deep-rooted feelings started to be unleashed as soon as it was apparent that authority had collapsed. One might say that some of those feelings were justified, as also was the need to calm them. As an example, it was fair to expect that black marketers, traitors, and collaborators should be on a black list and subject to punishment. It was also a big issue about women who had given themselves to the enemy either by will or by necessity for survival. These things were known by the people as to who among them was guilty. It was evident who was engaging in a given activity and why. Over time, behavior and actions formed patterns that neighbors could identify. The occupiers had injected themselves into the society and at times was difficult to avoid them. For example, had the German taken our home, and had we been able even to occupy the vacant lower wing (if he had allowed it), it would not have been possible to avoid him at all times. Neighbors would know, the same as we knew about our neighbors. Word got around in those days, to be sure. With regard to retributions, the problem was that the people raced without delay to satisfy their feelings and took matters in their own hands.

Often, their action was reprisal and not retribution. Therefore, this activity along with the existing ideological animosities, fueled the anarchy. The Greek authority soon to arrive and supported by the British contingent did not begin from zero, but rather from a point that was already in flames.

I have expressed my high sentiment for my father. We lost him six years after our return. He was sixty-two and I was in the US Army during the Korean conflict (I served in Germany and not in Korea at that time). Our family had experienced the entire saga of the war and the occupation of Greece. To enhance my description of that period, I will inject an excerpt from my website. I believe it will top off the whole account in a fitting way, concerning an American family at that time living in Greece. Reference is to my mother and the deep love she held for America. I expressed before, she may have gone close to her brothers and parents in Greece, a yearning she could not resist. Yet, she had carried America with her and never quit. The article follows:

LEGEND OF A FLAG

Legend has it that the American Flag was made by Elizabeth (Betsy) Ross. For a long time this was the public's prevailing belief, although unsupported entirely by any historical facts. It remains, however, as an inspiring and noble sentiment probably for most Americans. The story appears to have been started by William Canby, grandson of Betsy Ross. In a speech, he once made to the Pennsylvania Historical Society, he said General George Washington had consulted with Betsy Ross, a maker of flags, to plan the flag. It is possible, therefore, to believe that Betsy Ross was also the maker of the new Flag. In a separate story below, another American flag was made by an American, again to celebrate victory and freedom. This time, however, the event occurred under different circumstances outside of American soil but imbued the same sentiment.

DECLARATION

I, Demetra Klameris, widow of Marios Klameris and formerly a widow from my previous marriage to Constantine G. Karras, invoking the Name of God and being of sound mind, do hereby declare and testify of my own free will that the following described facts are true and authentic to the best of my memory and knowledge:

I and my husband, Constantine G. Karras, and our three children, who were born in Miami, Florida and whose names are George C. Karras, Athanassios C. Karras, and Constance C. Karras, resided in Athens, Greece (16, Anastassiou Tsocha, Ampelokipi). Together, as a family, we endured fully the bitter experience of the fall and subsequent occupation of Greece by the Axis forces in Wold War II, and we were stripped by the German occupation military authorities of our American passports and given instead substitute letters by the Swiss Red Cross in Athens, the said letters describing generally our status as U.S. citizens.

On the very day (October 1944), and moments after we witnessed the first British troops entering Athens in buses from Kifissias Avenue, arriving at Ampelokipi Terminus (Terma Ampelokipon), and turning right at Alexandras Avenue, while at the same time, and in plain view of all witnesses present, the German contingent staffing the nearby Ipokration Hospital departed in an orderly formation on Vassilissis Sofias Avenue in the direction of Syntagma Square, the said contingent marching on the very road which today lies in front of the Embassy of the United States of America, I and my family made and hoisted what may well have been the first American Flag to appear in Athens immediately after the occupation began to crumble.

We set out feverishly to prepare the Flag by using our few remaining white linen bed sheets. The most difficult task became the preparation of the Stars, not only because of their shape but also because of the need to have ninety-six pieces displayed on both sides of the blue field. I sewed the Flag with my own hands, proudly and with deep personal satisfaction completing the task within hours, while my family hovered over me pressing, impatiently, that I should do the job quickly. The Flag was eventually hung from a pole (an ordinary rounded piece of wood) and secured on the iron grill work of our third floor bedroom window (at Villa Dessylla, 18 Anastassiou Tsocha Street) and appeared prominently visible from various directions in the surrounding area.

Soon after the Flag was displayed, a committee of wandering liberation enthusiasts respectfully approached our home and requested to borrow the Flag in order to display it the following day at a planned Liberation Parade in the center of Athens, with the promise that the Flag would be returned to us at the end of what expectedly became one of a series of tumultuous events. The Flag was returned as promised, and remained hoisted for quite some time until both the blue and red colors eventually began to fade to a shade of sky-blue and pink, respectively, due to exposure and to the poor quality of dyes we were able to garner.

This historical Flag was eventually lost because of our speedy departure to the United States the following year.

It might be worthy to mention that, on one occasion during the civil upheaval of December 1944, which has been known as the "Bloody December," while British fighter planes dove low and strafed with machine gun fire the area of Ampelokipi, upon spotting the Flag, quickly interrupted their descent and waved their wings in greeting as they flew low over our home with a terrifying sound, soaring again high into the sky and returning from a different approach toward their target.

Along with my signature and testimony which appears above, my children are co-signing these presents as they, too, witnessed the events described above.

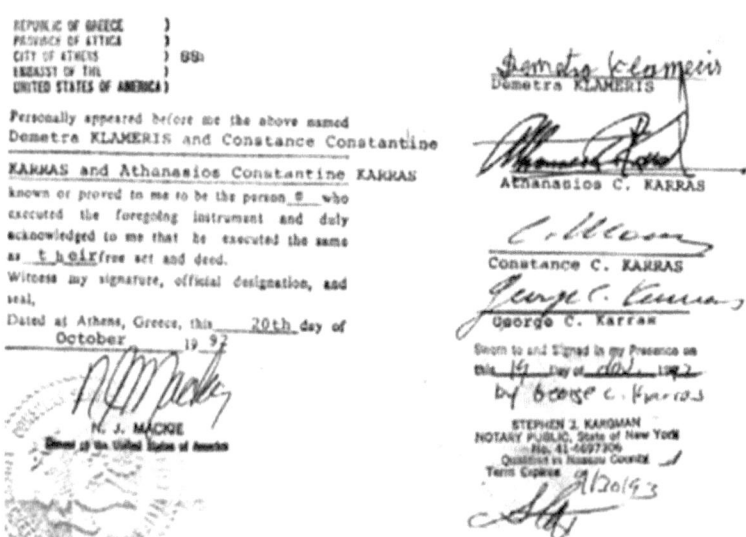

NOTE: The Athens Swiss Consulate and not the Swiss Red Cross is who issued the above cited Letter of Protection [Schutzbrief].

DEMETRA KARRAS KLAMERIS
nearest the age when she made an American Flag

This Declaration text and its anecdotal account executed and officially witnessed in 1992, along with personal photographs, are exclusive personal property and may not be emulated, reproduced, and distributed without authorized permission.

GEORGE A. LAZAROU
10, Lamias Street, Athens, 11523, Greece

AFFIDAVIT

I am George A. Lazarou a Greek citizen and I have resided at the above address in Ampelokipoi, Athens for my entire life. My father, Anastasios Lazarou, was the author of history text books for the established school system of Greece and I am the author of various books on American cinematography (e.g., *Images in Low Key – Cinematographer Sol Polito*).

As a childhood friend of the Karras brothers and with first hand and intimate knowledge of the Karras family, I hereby attest to the fact that the content of the *Declaration* of Demetra Klameris was personally typewritten by me at my residence and it is authentic and true as stated over her signature on October 20, 1992.

Attest: _____
GEORGE A. LAZAROU

REPUBLIC OF GREECE)
PROVINCE OF ATTICA)
CITY OF ATHENS) SS:
EMBASSY OF THE)
UNITED STATES OF AMERICA)

Subscribed and Sworn to
before me on September 29, 1998

John S. Tavenner
Consul of the United
States of America

_____

George A. Lazarou died April 8, 2012

Social upheaval in Greece has always existed. Otherwise, how could democracy have come into existence? It was a symptom of a prior cause and went on from there even until now. We have already established that principle of symptoms from causes. Yet, let's be real: is there any society that does not go through the same? Of course not. Only today, our focus is on Greece during the time that Fascism, Nazism, Communism and the like were in play. Ioannis Metaxas, as we have seen, became the dictator and was trying to imitate Mussolini, as Hitler did also. In essence then, in Greece there were opposing segments of the population—some leaning right and others left. This is enough to stir up a discord. And, as I am writing this account, look at the situation that prevails in the US today. We've gone through all of this already in previous pages: The Germans and the Italians are in Greece. Between them they agree to territorial spheres of influence. Overall, the Germans exert the bigger authority. There was more than enough friction between them. The Germans felt they deserved primacy, because they were the ones to pull the Italians out of the soup on the Albanian front. There were occasions when Germans fanned the fires of ridicule against the Italians. The Germans, of course, knew that they themselves were hated by the Greeks. They also knew the low esteem Greeks had for the Fascists, because in effect the Greeks had defeated them in Albania. So, what the Germans did is to use Greek anti-Italian humor against the Italians. This humiliated the Italians, but there was little they could do. And this produced a double humiliation, exposing the Italian inability to stop the flow of humor against them. On one well-known occasion at the Zapion center where there was a coffee shop and an orchestra-stand to entertain the public; the Germans compelled the orchestra to play a pre-invasion popular tune whose lyrics began with: "Hey, sucker Mussolini..."

This icy tie that existed between the Germans and the Italians did nothing to cool down the mounting heat between the Greek left and right. The matter became very complicated. Both Greek sides asserted themselves as patriots, because both had formed underground resistance against the Germans and the Italians.

That is one point. The other point is that of the two, the left had achieved a more definite profile as the leading force struggling for the liberation of Greece. Be that as it may, it is not that the other side lacked in their dedication. Where it all got sticky is in the ideologies involved. The left was fighting for the liberation of Greece, but in the process, it was also interjecting its Marxist ideology. That's pretty heavy stuff. My uncle (the one who was first to enter the recaptured Argyrokastron), had walked home all the way from Albania, because there was no transportation for the retreating soldiers. He stayed not in Athens, but in the ancestral settlement in the mountains we discussed—although he went to Athens on occasion. He was the school-teacher of that settlement. Well, the underground demanded his participation. He could not reconcile the ideology thrust upon him. It was resolved that he be executed. Now, how can that be? Was one to be a patriot? Or, was one to be a Communist? It could not be synonymous; therefore, it was a puzzle. It is true that the main thrust of the left underground did fight the Germans. The question is always: Which motivated them the most? The desire to liberate? Or, the desire to have a Marxist Greece after it was liberated? The quandary is that those five people who were hanged (at the time of my incident with the German) were at once both left-leaning guerillas and patriots. I went back to that spot more than once to honor them. I took my wife there to witness. Let me put it this way: That German was not my friend. He might have killed me that day. The people who were hanged were fighting that German. No matter what my ideology might be; am I not to value those people? Also, let's not forget, that one or more of them may have been free of ideology and in their mind only fighting for liberation. And in the final analysis, these were Greeks who perished that way. There was much confusion in that period. Besides my uncle, there were boyhood friends who lived up in the mountain settlements. They had been recruited in the ranks, and their unit had come down to Athens in trucks. They served, in their opinion, as patriots; but, they had also been indoctrinated. I knew many persons and their diverse convictions. Also, I knew the leading person of the cell in our area. They were good people with families and with different viewpoints. And that was the source of the confusion that then turned into progressive disagreement that ended in hatred and bloodshed. That was the one side.

The other side had its own ideology. This generated friction. The Greek government working under the Germans was right-leaning, and this accommodated the Germans who were fighting Communism. But, this also rendered that government as collaborationist, even though the object was to serve Greece. The clash became more and more intensified. The British were involved, and their interest was against the left. It's odd, because that would seem to help the Germans. Churchill at one time found himself in the predicament of ordering the elimination of left-side demonstrators who, after all, were fighting for the liberation of Greece. The country found itself in this kind of situation very soon after the liberation. Talks of cooperation broke down in December 1944 and the struggle started full-fledged, with the British also involved and being in the cross-hairs of the left side. We kept flying the American flag my mother had made. Our home was south of Alexandras, and we were considered to be on the Nationalist side. The side across was considered to be the left-leaning side, or the EAM (acronym for Greek Liberation Front) side. This division did not mean that everybody living across from us favored the left. For example, my grandparents' home was on that side. What had happened is that the left underground had crossed Alexandras and established itself there. Alexandras had become the border and thus a no-man's land. The front gate of our home faced south, while the back of the house was north toward Alexandras. The back and sides of the property were all surrounded by a tall stone-built fence. The front was enclosed by a mid-height stone wall lined on top with an ornate heavy metal fence, and the heavy gate we talked about. The place gave much privacy, as can be imagined. And there was garden growth all around and fruit trees. The back also had a good size well from which water could be drawn by hand or pump.

Standing in the front of the south side of our home, which
faced the front gate. My sister and my life-long friend on her
right (he certified that my mother's declaration was true).
I am on her left.

I describe all this for events that will be covered later. Besides
the three floors, there was also a basement in the house. On the left
side of the garden, when entering the property was a separate small
building with a two-car garage on the right and living quarters for
the gardener on the left. Part of the rent paid for the gardener. In
closing, none of this exists any longer. A multistory government
building is there today.

The time is December 1944. The Germans are gone. The
British are in Greece. For me and everybody else, the occupation
is over. In the last three and one-half years getting around and
visiting has been minimal. I got the notion to go visit an uncle on
my mother's side. Neither we nor his family had news about the
other. The uncle was a stately grey-headed gentleman, soft-spoken
and kind. With my aunt, they had two sons whom in the early
years I always admired. They were a bit older than I, but disposed
to accept my younger company. My uncle was a parliamentarian
in the Greek government. For that matter, both brothers also rose
to prominence in their own right. One was a submariner in the
Greek navy and became an admiral (he was once blinded during an

operation but recovered. Another time he was at the US Naval Base in Key West, Florida and he had come to Miami to be my best man at my wedding). The other brother served as Greek ambassador in Holland and Washington, DC. For some reason, I had developed a strong yearning to go visit them. They lived in one of the big apartment complexes across from the Columns of Olympian Zeus near Syntagma Square. It's a nice location of the city even today. Whenever I played soccer, that is where I went with my friends and classmates. There is wide space at the very base of those columns that served the purpose. I don't know if the authorities allow this type of activity any longer. They try to preserve the integrity of the ancient sites. Mazower's book has an illustration showing a German antiaircraft armored vehicle posted there. What a disgrace! What a contradiction of cultures! Of course, the cowards that they were: The Nazis posted their weapon at that location, knowing that the Allied aircraft would not bomb or machine-gun the ancient precious site. So, they took shelter under the power they claimed as weaker than their own. Such pathetic, shameless cowards! The walk from my home was quite lengthy, but I did a lot of it anyway. It was now something I could do with no Germans and Italians around. There was activity as a result of new-found freedom. The day of my visit was quite soon after a major demonstration and shooting that took place at Syntagma Square. That incident had historical importance. It happened the day after the breakdown of the reconciliation talks I mentioned earlier. On one side was the ELAS (Greek Popular Liberation Army), which was the armed component of EAM (the major underground administrative and ideological left movement in Greece). On the other side was the provisional government of Greece, which was on the right in its ideology and favored by Britain etc. The talks were about disarming the ELAS. The ELAS refused to disarm and the talks broke down. The next day, 3 December 1944, a large demonstration by EAM took place at Syntagma Square. The police for some unknown reason opened fire on the demonstrators. It is a question whether this was because police feared things were getting out of hand, or fear of a government takeover, or if it was provoked. Whatever the reason, the match was lit. That was the day that Greece was thrust into civil war. The immediate reaction of the underground was to begin retaliation by attacking the police stations in Athens (it sounds familiar, considering the US today as I write this). Commotions and reports about them had become commonplace—again refer to callousness and being acclimated to it all—not ever without fear and anxiety, of course. In any event, I was still bent on going to visit my uncle and his family. To get there, one must reach Syntagma Square and then onward a bit more. First, one would pass by the National Garden. When I neared the garden, a stench of death hit me. There must have been dead bodies in there hidden from public view and left there to decay. It was a shock to experience that, knowing how beautiful the place used to be in the prewar years. It was a signal for me to expect that nothing any more would be what it was before. I began to wonder what surprise I would find with my uncle's family. I got there and went up and knocked on the door, and when they saw me they were stunned. In their face was written: What in the world are you doing here? First of all, the two brothers were not there. I believe they had taken precautions to safeguard. My uncle must have had information about pending things to happen. I had not met with any trouble getting to their home. Their urging was for me to get out of that area at once. They dispensed with niceties and told me to go right away. They would not invite me to stay because they were uncertain about their own situation. I did as they said. I hurried out of their apartment building and rushed into the street to go home. I was too late. I was out in a very open space in the road. I aimed to the nearest street I saw and dashed toward it. I could see an officer and a subordinate dragging a typical x-shaped wood frame wrapped with barbed wire used in blockades. A line of them were already in place. This was the last one and they were rushing to close it. I ran, but I never would have made it. I couldn't have processed in my mind what I did, because I was running, I was excited, and frantic. Yet, it was immediate: I started yelling in English for them to let me through. I was near enough by then to hear the officer shout at the other man, "What's this one? What's he saying?" Meanwhile, they were both dragging that unit as fast as they could to shut it. They had no mind to favor me. They couldn't care less. They were looking to get out of there themselves. The other man yelled back, "I think he's speaking English." It only took a second for the officer to say, "Let him pass." The other man held back from pulling and gave me a chance to just squeeze through. They closed it up right away, and they too sprinted away. I had heard shooting come from behind me. There is tree-growth and vegetation in that area, and I believe it came from there—the shooting was aimed our way. This kind of activity went on all over. Pandora's box had been opened wide and all the venom and hatred gathered in people's heart in the past years was pouring out. What with the collaborating security forces and the terror and atrocities they had committed; what with the exploiters and traitors; and what with ideological anger that existed, the county was in turmoil. Personal scores too were being settled as part of the overall condition.

It was not uncommon to be confronted by lone-wolf situations—individuals who took advantage of the instability that prevailed. Another incident happened around the corner near our house. My brother and I were returning home one evening, having visited our grandparents. It was a moonless night. We had crossed Alexandras walking south toward our street, where we would turn left a brief walk to our front gate. In other words, we were just around the corner from our house. All at once, out of nowhere, what appeared to be three or four individuals surrounded us. It was pitch dark and only their silhouettes showed. One of them pressed a handgun in my belly, and another did the same to my brother. A demanding and firm voice asked: "What are you? Communists or Nationalists? Our reaction was identical. We both said, "Communists." The voice responded, "All right comrades, go on." Our spontaneous response was tailored to the setting.

These incidents were not jokes. Blood was boiling and being spilled in those days. Had we contradicted each other, or had we said Nationalists, our parents and our sister would have witnessed two corpses on the pavement the next morning. Unbelievable you say? Witness today, radical Islamic terrorism. That particular time of the upheaval was labeled, "Dekemvriana" (meaning, December doings); which has earned an even more descriptive title, "Bloody December." Often conditions were seen as worse than those of the occupation, depending, of course, on the personal experience of the individual. The crisis came to an end with an agreement reached on 12 February 1945.

Things continued to simmer and in 1946 erupted again into a second full-fledged civil war until 1949. I returned home to the US in September 1945. My account can only refer to the events I experienced during that ominous December. Clashes became ferocious, scattered, and unpredictable. Danger could come from any angle and for no good reason. A sniper could be lurking in some window looking for opportunity targets—for the cause he served or for fun. No guerilla in his right mind would be staying on the Nationalist side shooting his weapon and risking being discovered. His elimination would be instant. Yet, shooting came from the south, directed north into the third-floor bedroom window that faced south. In other words, it came from the Nationalist side. Someone was practicing his long-distance shooting skills as a sport. One bullet missed my brother by no more than an inch or two, when it penetrated the back of the chair, went through the sturdy wooden bedroom door, and lodged itself in the wall. He was hanging his jacket on the back of that chair. I was in the walk-in closet and heard the racket that thing made. I ran into the bedroom and saw him standing there, petrified. Do not assume that this was a single incident. Not at all. Yet, it was from the north beyond Alexandras that the torrent of bullets came. Let me describe what was going on.

It is evident that the house we lived in was prominent in the area due to its height and its size. It was for good reason that the German had wanted to throw us out and take it over. Number one, he would have enjoyed it, and very well bragged to his peers how well he was accommodated. Number two, he would have had a near complete visual command of the area around the house and long distance. The height of the building was one reason, and the other was the number of windows all around the third floor, and the door to the terrace. Also, there was limited number of tall buildings to block his far view. Number three, it was an ideal location to set up weaponry for the strategic control of that whole area in all directions. Furthermore, the house lent itself to much attention in terms of how it could be used in other ways (German social activities and such), if first it was neutralized—and by that, I mean eliminating prior residents first. To add yet another feature; although the house was not on a main thoroughfare, it was located in a place that offered convenient access to it. This whole combination of features had placed us in a horrible position. To complete the scene, almost everybody came through the house, compounding the danger of being there.

First of all, it was winter and it was cold. Snow in Attica was occasional; but the cold was very penetrating and I remember chapped hands and lips. When all the random shootings and unpredictable marauding started, we took shelter in the basement below. In recent times, the owner had brought in two young-middle-age couples friends of his to occupy the vacant first floor. The Swiss couple had left some time ago. The four of them, the five of us, and the gardener were the only ones who by right should be there. Wrong. That was wartime. Things were never normal. Some fifteen-sixteen people (more or less, as it varied) ended up being in there. They had sought shelter, and it is obvious they couldn't have been refused. People needed safety. This was not every day, but it did happen. British aircraft were flying overhead, attacking and machine-gunning the guerillas across from Alexandras. The large caliber ejected cartridges were dropping down making a bell-like sound when hitting the ground. It would be insanity to be outside when this was going on. We could see them from the basement window as they came from the southern direction. They were not the only passer-by. There was a constant fluttering sound of the artillery shells going overhead. Meanwhile, the house was being shot at by guerillas from the other side, suspecting that national military or the British were posted there.

This sort of thing became very frequent that month of December. First what happened is that a unit of resistance guerillas numbering three hundred entered Athens, and as we know attacked the police stations. I cannot know what their strategy was regarding their moves. One thing is clear, they shifted from the center of town northward toward Ampelokipi. Their aim was to reach the northern part of that area across from Alexandras, which rose in elevation.

It is reasonable to believe that either some of them had gotten up there already; or it was local sympathizers who were shooting at us; even before the main body of the guerillas arrived there. Either way, we had to be holed up in the basement. It was very cold one day and we had gone down in a great hurry. After a while, it became a need for somebody to go upstairs and bring overcoats. It was my father and I who went. We hurried up the marble steps to the veranda, went into the house, got the garments and rushed back down. I'm following my father as we reach the stairwell outside the veranda. The stairway down faced south toward the front gate. Lo and behold, just in front of us in single file, on their bellies, dragging themselves on the driveway all the way from the front gate are guerillas armed to the teeth. The moment they saw us, as we made our sudden appearance, two or three of them in front lifted themselves up and pointed their guns at us. It was like a cobra rising and ready to strike. The immediate reaction of my father was, "Greeting to you, brave ones" (I must admit the Greek unique expression cannot be imitated, "Yassas Pallikaria"). When they heard that, their tension was relaxed, they pulled down their guns, and continued on their way to the north end of the property. They spent much time there. They were reluctant even to climb over the wall. They wanted to stay low, and I know why very well—a line of men that long would soon become obvious. Instead, they dug a hole at the base of that thick stone wall and went through it. By that night, they were all gone except for one man who stayed behind. At first, he stayed holed up in the gardener's room next to the garage. Then, he decided to join us in the basement. It was clear that his action was not because he had some ideological change of heart, shifting his loyalties to the other side. Plain and simple, he was fed up with what he was doing and he saw a chance to escape it all. He stayed in the basement with us, never for a moment separating himself from his rifle. None of us showed any ill feeling toward him, and at the same time there was no social interaction at all. It was an uncomfortable situation. He was not a big fellow, but he looked strong and healthy. His clothing seemed to be good enough to keep him warm. His rifle, which seemed big for his size, never left him. It was obvious he was AWOL. We did share food with him. He remained with us in the basement until we all came out. It was the usual practice: When things quieted down outside, we would leave the basement and go about our activities. His presence and the weapon he held had everyone on edge. He too was not at ease and always out of place. He was not comfortable being there. Even though we scattered, he kept an eye on one or more of us at all times even from a distance. Things were peaceful for some time Then, all of a sudden, he started yelling for everybody to come outside in the open. It was odd, because none of us had even thought or planned to attack or disarm him. We were all just sitting it out. He lined everybody up facing him, pointed his rifle at us and moved it left and right, as though to include us all, and started screaming, "All right, who shot at me, who?" He said that several times, then quieted down and decided to release us. The man was not insane. Someone must have shot at him, wherever he may have been at the time. I did not hear any bullet impact somewhere, nor did anyone else, but he did. I believe that. And I also believe that some lone sniper was the shooter. I say this because of my brother's incident on the third-floor. And also because of another time I never mentioned, when standing at the front gate, my brother and I were fired upon somewhere from the south direction. The gate was not visible from anywhere in the north, except from our house. The case with that fellow ended as quick as it had started. That night he decided to give it up. He left through the hole in the back wall, the same as the rest did. As I stated earlier, the house had become a transit depot. It is true. First was the German who wanted to take it over. Then, there were the neighbors who came and went at their pleasure. Next, it was the guerillas passing through en masse with at least one guest for a while. And not to forget the French and Swiss diplomats and the two middle-age couples. Nonetheless it is not done yet. The American flag up on the third-floor window must have had a play in this—calling people to come in.

My mother's brother, the teacher, having learned about the intentions of the guerillas, fled the settlement and came to Athens. He stayed with my grandparents as expected. For a while his safety was assured. That changed when the guerillas took over the section north of Alexandras. The danger was renewed. He risked an escape one night and succeeded coming across. Dragged himself low on the ground, and reached our back wall. By good fortune he fell upon the very hole the guerillas had carved out. He wormed through it and then appeared in our home to the great surprise and delight of all of us. The irony of it was that he had escaped one major danger, only to come to another with all of the fire we were subjected to. We would gather in the two rooms on the second-floor and avoid the third-floor. But, even there, safety was questionable. To lower the risk, we had taken the metal lid off the large water deposit on the terrace and placed it against the window of the dining-room. That window faced north and it was a target for those shooting at us. We also ran up a mattress against the lid to add thickness. The bullets would come into the room and ricochet around us. No one was hurt. I picked up some mangled bullets off the floor, and I still have them as a...souvenir. The north side was battered all the time. We were in the basement one day. As I recall, my mother had put beans to boil (beans were a standard for nourishment and a luxury food if they could be found; and olive oil, the Greek gold, was even more difficult or impossible to get) and she wanted to run upstairs to check. The kitchen, of course, was on the second floor. A door on the north side of the kitchen opened to a metal escape-stairway right outside. The door was half window half door. From that window, one could see the well nearby in the back, pump and all. We had managed to sneak up to the kitchen, and as my mother was stirring the pot, a mortar shell came in, struck the well and demolished it and the pump. The glass panes in the window were all shattered, the door/window combination was blown open. How we did not receive shrapnel or glass injury is a very big mystery. It was the worst of its kind compared to all other shelling. I looked at my mother, she looked at me, and neither one was hurt. By all accounts, my mother had become a combat veteran. There was no doubt, that the frequency of those events made life unreal. And surviving such circumstances was something unique to have happened. Next thing, we are visited by an officer of the Greek forces that had uniforms closer in style to the Allies than to that of the Greek troops at the start of the war. Even their cigarettes had that specific aroma of the English stock. They were equipped in the

Allied fashion. He led a small squad of some eight or so men. He announced that they would be quartered in our home. Well, that was the final touch. Our last visitor had arrived, but this time with bells on. They came in full gear, all their equipment and all sorts of weaponry. And as I had always thought, they went straight up to the master-bedroom window (from where I used to observe the guerilla activities far up north of Alexandras, with a telescope my radio friend had given me—he had another one his engineer uncle had given him) and they set up a machine gun. There you have it. The house was now converted to a front-line military post. The mess, of course, as one can imagine, was complete. I still remember the despair in my mother's face, when at first in false hope she thought she could keep her home in order. She soon adapted to the reality and I admired her for that. Her stoicism outmatched it all. Kudos.

RETURN TO AMERICA

In the end, there was only one thing that was left for all of us to do. And that was to be grateful. And, by all of us I do not mean our family alone. I mean every single soul that came through there—people of all stripes, friends and enemies, civilians and military, partisans and neutrals, and whatever else applies. Consider this: In spite of all that happened in and around that home, with so many people milling about, with all the shootings intentional and stray, with shelling and explosions, with bullets ricocheting in and out and all around—not one single casualty, not even a scratch, took place. The only victim registered was a set of Czechoslovakian crystal glassware that my parents had put away in a trunk and kept in the walk-in closet upstairs. That, along with some fine china got hit by a stray bullet that went through the trunk. Even so, the damage was minimal. Only few pieces of each set were struck. Both sets are still in possession of our current family as a thankful reminder of the final victory of those days.

In time, things stared to normalize. The military, of course, moved out of our home. We began putting our life together, both at home and outside. We started a feverish effort to secure our American identity. The American Consulate at that time was housed near the National Garden (the park cleaned up, of course) on Vassilissis Sofias. There were several friendships developed with the British soldiers who were anxious for a bit of relief from their stark military life. Yet as expected, they were all happy friendships, but short-lived, given the mobility of the military. My serious concern became to recover from the delay in completing my school requirements. So, I kept up whenever possible. I was also aware at the time of my own need to share in the recovery of our family in various ways. I had heard that there was an American presence established at the Eleusis airfield outside of Athens (yes, the place of the Eleusinian Mysteries of ancient times—almost every spot in Greece has some history to tell); and that the American military trucks shuttled back and forth to Omonia Square with American personnel. I went there and waited for several hours. A truck did come as alleged, and American military personnel jumped off and scattered around. I approached and told them that I am an American. One of them at once told me to follow him. Right there, in Omonia Square, on the second floor of a building with a wide glass-window frontage facing the square (still there), was an office. An American captain heard the man tell him what I was. He hired me on the spot. Told the man to take me to the truck before it left. I climbed up, and next thing I was at the Eleusis airfield. It was the US Air Transport Command and I was given a job as supply-room clerk, first for food and then for clothing. My assignment was a rotation of three days on and three off. I didn't show up at home until three days later. With things the way they were still unstable, the family was frantic. All that though took a quick turn when they knew what happened; and when I started emptying some bags with chocolates, coffee, sugar, and cookies. From then on, it all took shape. The biggest problem I had was to reconcile my schedule with school attendance—unheard of in the Greek austere education system, not to be a hundred percent student. I do not know how it is today.

Nevertheless, all the paperwork was put in place, including school records, citizenship, passage on board the Gripsholm (a Swedish ship ferrying back home American prisoners of war and expatriates from Asia and Europe). My brother and I were the first two in the family to make the trip. We traveled from Piraeus to Haifa, Alexandria, Naples, Marseilles, and New York. Expatriates had to pay for the cost of the trip, and on arrival home were also visited by the FBI to protect against intrusion by foreign agents.

The question arises: How close to that is the practice today? And if not, why not? Upon our arrival, the great Lady in New York harbor was waiting: Welcome home!

My brother (left) and I, walking free ... back to America on the deck of the Gripsholm in 1945.

The rest is irrelevant for what concerns this writing.

It was late in life for me to do this. Yet, here it is.

God save America from the scourge of corruption and evil.

EVENT MAP

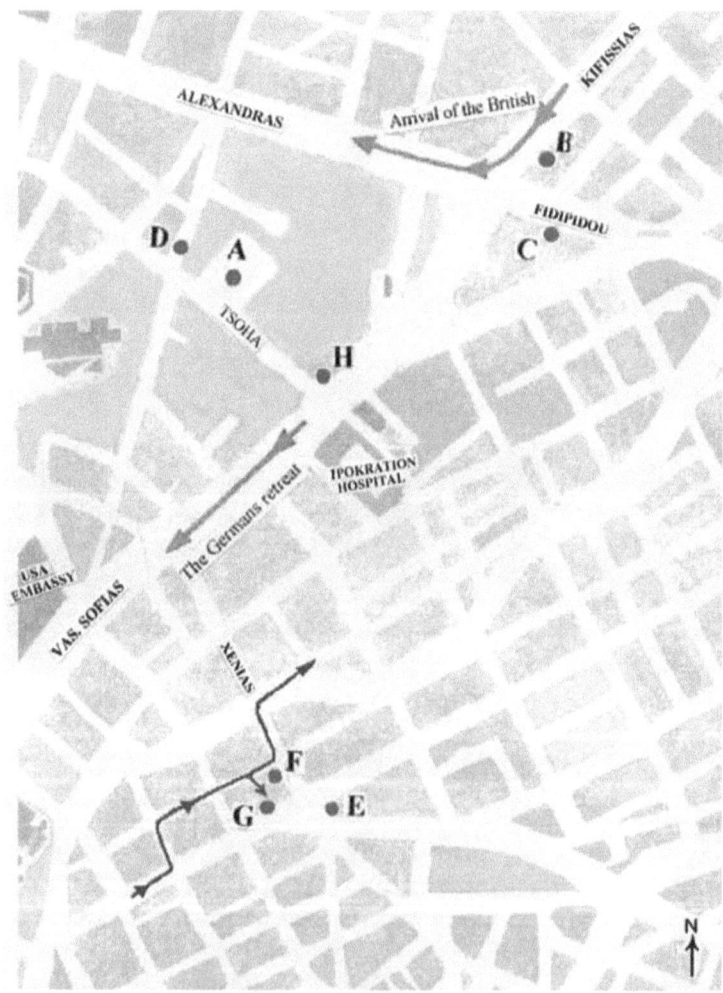

Refer to the index below for explanation of the letters
A to H in the Map.

EVENT INDEX

A ... Our Home.

B ... Lot where the first two German open-top personnel vehicles parked.

C ... Location of the surrender of Athens.

D ... My brother and I ambushed by the Communists at night.

E ... Corner where five resistance fighters were hanged by the Germans.

F ... Corner where I was ambushed by the German.

G ... My friend's home (arrow shows our trajectory from school and my escape).

H ... My position from where I witnessed both the British and the Germans.

A CLOSING NOTE

DESPITE THE AUTHOR'S HARSH experience early in his life, his positive outlook never diminished. To the contrary, it was enhanced further and firmed up. The reader may also wish to refer to the following from the author:

BOOK
Amazon, Goodreads, eBay:
Seven Gates to Freedom:
Awareness & Consciousness

WEBSITES
https://www.aylahesperia.com

https://www.New-Byzantium.org/

Author INTERVIEW
(live video)
https://www.youtube.com/watch?v=fEsFgeVjKO0

WWII DEFINING QUOTES

Does the world once again owe gratitude to Greece?

Had Russia fallen to the Nazi juggernaut, it is considered that Germany would well have ruled the entire globe.
Shown below is the evidence that due to the heroic resistance of the Greek nation against the Nazi and Fascist war machine, precious time was given to Russia to rise and to defeat the enemy. Greece's delay against the Axis had a multiplier effect, giving time to the Alliance of the West to prepare and thus to gain the decisive upper hand. The American Pacific victory may have had a much different outcome if the European theater had been encumbered with a Russian defeat.

Franklin Roosevelt
President of the United States of America:

"On the 28th of October 1940 Greece was given a deadline of three hours to decide on war or peace but even if a three day or three week or three year were given, the response would have been the same. The Greeks taught dignity throughout the centuries. When the entire world had lost all hope, the Greek people dared to question the invincibility of the German monster raising against it the proud spirit of freedom."

(Paraphrased from speech he delivered on 10 Jun 1943)

"The heroic struggle of the Greek people ... against Germany's attack, after she so thunderously defeated the Italians in their attempt to invade the Greek soil, filled the hearts of the American people with enthusiasm and moved their compassion."

(Paraphrased from a speech of his on 25 Apr 1941)

Winston Churchill

"Until now we used to say that the Greeks fight like heroes. Now we shall say: The heroes fight like Greeks."

(From a speech he delivered from the BBC in the first days of the Greco-Italian war).

"The word heroism I am afraid does not render the least of those acts of self-sacrifice of the Greeks, which were the defining factor in the victorious outcome of the common struggle of the nations, during WWII, for the human freedom and dignity. If it were not for the bravery of the Greeks and their courage, the outcome of WWII would be undetermined."

(Paraphrased from one of his speeches to the British Parliament on 24 Apr 1941)

George VI, King of Great Britain

"The magnificent struggle of Greece, was the first big turn of WWII."

(Paraphrased from a speech of his to the parliament in May 1945)

Sir Robert Antony Eden
Minister of War and the Exterior of Britain
Prime Minister of Britain

"Regardless of what the future historians shall say, what we can say now, is that Greece gave Mussolini an unforgettable lesson, that she was the motive for the revolution in Yugoslavia, that she held the Germans in the mainland and in Crete for six weeks, that she upset the chronological order of all German High Command's plans and thus brought a general reversal of the entire course of the war and we won."

(Paraphrased from a speech of his to the British parliament
on 24 Sep 1942)

Sir Harold Leofric George Alexander
British Marshal during WWII

"It would not be an exaggeration to say that Greece upset the plans of Germany in their entirety forcing her to postpone the attack on Russia for six weeks. We wonder what would have been Soviet Union's position without Greece."

(Paraphrased from a speech of his to the British parliament
on 28 Oct 1941)

Joseph Vissarionovich Tzougasvili Stalin

"I am sorry because I am getting old and I shall not live long to thank the Greek People, whose resistance decided WWII."

(From a speech of his broadcast by the Moscow radio station
on 31 Jan 1943 after the victory of Stalingrad and the
capitulation of marshal Paulus)

Georgy Constantinovich Zhoucov
Marshal of the Soviet Army

"If the Russian people managed to raise resistance at the doors of Moscow, to halt and reverse the German torrent, they owe it to the Greek People, who delayed the German divisions during the time they could bring us to our knees."

(Quote from his memoirs on WWII)

Moscow Radio Station

"You fought unarmed and won, small against big. We owe you gratitude, because you gave us time to defend ourselves. As Russians and as people we thank you."

Charles de Gaul

"I am unable to give the proper breadth of gratitude I feel for the heroic resistance of the People and the leaders of Greece."

(From a speech of his to the French Parliament after the end of WWII)

Maurice Schumann
Minister of the exterior of France
Member of the French Academy

"Greece is the symbol of the tortured, bloodied but live Europe. Never a defeat was so honorable for those who suffered it."

(From a message of his he addressed from the BBC of London to the enslaved peoples of Europe on 28 Apr 1941, the day Hitler occupied Athens)

Adolf Hitler
"For the sake of historical truth I must verify that only the Greeks, of all the adversaries who confronted us, fought with bold courage and highest disregard of death."

(From a speech to the Reichstag on 4 May 1941)

Benito Mussolini
"The war with Greece proved that nothing is firm in the military and that surprises always await us."

(From speech he delivered on 10 May 1941)

FACTS OF RECORD

DURATION OF RESISTANCE (in days):

Greece 219
Norway 61
France 43 (The superpower at the time)
Poland 30
Belgium 18
Holland 4
Yugoslavia 3
Czechoslovakia 0
Luxemburg 0
Denmark 0 (The Danes surrendered to Hitler's motorcyclist who was conveying Hitler's request to the Danish king for the crossing of the Nazi armies. The Danish king indicating submission surrendered his crown to the motorcyclist).

TOTAL GREEK CASUALTIES IN WWII BY COUNTRY:

Albanians killed 1,165 Greeks
Italians killed 8,000 Greeks
Bulgarians killed 25,000 Greeks
Germans killed 50,000 Greeks

TOTAL LOSES IN POPULATION PERCENTAGES:

Greece 10%
Soviet Union 2.8%
Holland 2.2%
France 2% (The superpower at the time)
Poland 1.8%
Yugoslavia 1.7%
Belgium 1.5%

GREECE FOUGHT FOUR ENEMIES AT THE SAME TIME:

Albania
Bulgaria
Germany
Italy

On 10 April 1941, after the capitulation to Germany, the northern forts of Greece surrender. The Germans express their admirations to Greek soldiers, declare that they were honored and proud to have as their adversary such an army and request that the Greek commandant inspect the German army in a demonstration of honor and recognition! The German flag is raised only after the complete withdrawal of the Greek army. A German officer of the air force declared to the commander of the Greek Eastern Macedonia division group, lieutenant general Dedes that the Greek army was the first army on which the Stuka fighter planes did not cause panic. "Your soldiers" he said, "instead of fleeing frantically, as they did in France and Poland, were shooting at us from their positions."

The Greeks initially surrendered only to the Germans. Mussolini demanded that the Greek Army also surrender to Italy! He continued attacks against the Greeks during their surrender to the Germans. Yet, the Greeks once again defeated the Italians. Hitler, to help Mussolini save face, urged General Dietrich to prevail upon General Georgios Tsolakoglou who included defeated Italy in the surrender ...

OXI!–NO! 28 October 1940

Source: Greece_In_World_War_II.pps [*Kythera Family*]

WHAT'S IN A LIFE

Title: What's in a Life

Author: Mark Athanasios C. Karras

Publisher: Karras

ISBN: 979-8-89216-004-9 (Paperback)
979-8-89216-005-6 (Ebook)

Pages: 124

Genre: Memoir

Reviewed by: David Allen

What's in a Life is a heartfelt memoir, truly epic in scope. It not only captures the complex personal shadings of occupied wartime life, but makes intelligible the huge historic events of 1941-5 in Greece and beyond.

Greece, long the standard bearer for civilization, free thought, and democracy, suffered mightily but courageously, fighting off successive invasions by Mussolini's Fascists, Hitler's Wehrmacht, and by the subsequent incursions of Greek civil war between the Nationalists vs. Communists.

In each theater of war, the author, his family, his people, showed their true colors: blue and white, sure, but also brave, dignified, and free all over. In the telling, the anecdotes, foibles and fatuities of combatants and bystanders both are highlighted in bold—readers will feel as though they are in the hands of a master storyteller.

Making sense out of nonsense; out of the irrational, out of history—this is the task of the writer, the memoir-maker. The writer functions here as translator, deciphering the cold crude events of today that end up being fractals of so much which has come before. Author Mark Athanasios C. Karras, most reasonably, would have us learn the lessons of the past, lest we repeat them. His description of the German occupation of Athens is global, fitful, chilling: he describes how every sector of life, from breadmaking to couturier to finding shelter, is grievously impacted by the sullen impossible presence of the Hun. The narrative actually soars at times, putting one very much in mind of occupied Paris as described in Mark Helprin's Paris in the Present Tense, and Ronald C. Rossbottom's When Paris Went Dark. Each récit conveys the horror, intrusiveness and damnable is-ness of having an enemy in one's backyard (not to mention parlor.)

The Karras' back story is of more than passing interest. Turns out that the family made it to the States but the paperwork was problematic and they had to return to Greece—at the worst of all possible times, smack dab in the middle of the Nazi invasion. Let there be no doubt: Karras' father was a hero. Not only did he learn French, but he made a self-taught effort to translate Edgar Allen Poe into Greek. The other hero in the book is the author's cool, wry sensibility, which he maintains throughout. He sums it up nicely, discussing how, in life, certain formulas always apply:

"[Be] ...Idle and you will fail; rush and you will stumble; study and you will learn; try and you will gain; lie and you will rue; respect and you will be respected ...When time is used with wisdom, the outcome is ...good."

This read about this man's life in time is very, very good.

www.ingramcontent.com/pod-product-compliance
Lightning Source LLC
Chambersburg PA
CBHW030317130626
46549CB00002B/895